The Complete Illustrated Manual of Handgun Skills

The Complete Illustrated Manual of Handgun Skills

Robert Campbell

ZENITH PRESS

First published in 2011 by Zenith Press, an imprint of MBI Publishing Company, 400 First Avenue North, Suite 300, Minneapolis, MN 55401 USA

Zenith Press titles are also available at discounts in bulk quantity for industrial or sales-promotional use. For details write to Special Sales Manager at MBI Publishing Company, 400 First Avenue North, Suite 300, Minneapolis, MN 55401 USA.

To find out more about our books, join us online at www.zenithpress.com.

Library of Congress Cataloging-in-Publication Data

Campbell, R. K. (Robert K.), 1958-

The complete illustrated manual of handgun skills / Robert Campbell.

    p. cm.

ISBN 978-0-7603-4105-6 (sb : alk. paper)

1. Pistols. 2. Revolvers. 3. Shooting. I. Title.

GV1153.C236 2010

683.4'3--dc22

                    2010045917

About the Author:

Robert Campbell, a former peace officer with over two decades on the job, has published more than six hundred articles, columns, and reviews in the firearms, personal defense, and outdoors field. His work appears in *Gun Week*, *Women and Guns*, *Gun List*, *Gun Digest*, *Handguns*, *Shotgun News*, *SWAT*, *Police*, *Tactical Gear*, *Concealed Carry Magazine*, *Handloader*, and other publications.

Design Manager: Brenda C. Canales
Designer: Helena Shimizu
Cover photo: Corean Komarec

All photographs are from the author's collection unless noted otherwise.

On the cover: Handguns, clockwise from top right: Ruger Blackhawk Convertible, Smith & Wesson 642 Airweight, CZ 75B with Kadet kit.

On the frontispiece: Smith & Wesson break-top revolver with Percival holster.

On the back cover: Main: The Beretta 92 on a firing range.

Inset: The author's customized Colt .45 with personalized holster.

Printed in China

10 9 8 7 6 5 4 3 2 1

Contents

Preface 7

Introduction: A Brief History of the Handgun 9

PART I: DIFFERENT TYPES OF RECREATIONAL HANDGUNS

Chapter 1: Single-Action Revolvers:
The Cowboy Way 21

Chapter 2: Trigger-Cocking Revolvers 35

Chapter 3: Mauser to Browning:
The First Self-Loaders............................ 47

Chapter 4: Automatics:
The Modern Self-Loaders 59

Chapter 5: Revolvers: The Best of the
Modern Revolvers.................................... 73

Chapter 6: General-Purpose Handguns.................... 85

PART II: BEFORE YOU BEGIN

Chapter 7: Methods of Operation 99

Chapter 8: Safety.. 113

Chapter 9: Marksmanship.. 123

Chapter 10: The First Handgun 135

PART III: RECREATIONAL HANDGUN TRAINING

Chapter 11: Just Making Brass.....................147

Chapter 12: Competition Shooting...........157

Chapter 13: Hunting 169

Chapter 14: Personal Defense....................179

PART IV: MAINTENANCE AND CUSTOMIZATION

Chapter 15: Taking Care of Your Handgun 201

Chapter 16: Materials and Finishes..........................211

Chapter 17: Accessories...221

Chapter 18: Ammunition and Handloading 237

Appendix: Ammunition Loads..................................247

Preface

WHEN I WAS EMBARRASSINGLY YOUNG I began firing and testing any handgun I could get my hands on. My family, cousins, my father, and my grandfathers, even my great grandfather and my mother indulged my interest. They supervised me closely but trusted a responsible child. By the time I was twelve years old I had taken small game with a handgun.

I lived in a rural area and was able to find a place to practice safely. My grandmother cooked the game I took. I began with the .22, and then experimented with the .32, taking squirrels with a Colt Detective Special in .32 Colt New Police caliber, and then I moved on to the .38 Special. In my world all was well. As time went by I learned of the efficiency of the .22 Magnum and I learned to handload the .38 Special. I discovered the writings of the great men of the day. You might say they were the Bishops of the Establishment or more accurately, Elmer Keith was the Bishop, Jeff Cooper the Priest, and Skeeter Skelton the Rector. Bill Jordan and Tom Ferguson were laymen. At least that was how I arranged it all in my mind.

In death no writer has been more elevated than Cooper, and none have deserved this reverence more than he. Some of the young lions have succumbed to commercialism and opted for small bores and plastic pistols, but that is okay for them and their personal worldview. Their infidelity to the great handguns and the big bore cartridges is disturbing, but they have only themselves to answer to. We do have a tendency to treasure untextured myths that affirm our preferred narrative. I prefer reality, however harsh a cup of coffee it may be. That is what you will find in this book: reality.

My early fascination was with any handgun, but as I progressed physically, financially, and mentally, I began to recognize quality and ability. I discovered something like alchemy. Handloading my own cartridges took the sting out of Magnums. I could load light loads. Conversely, handloading increased the efficiency of the small bores by maximizing the caliber. I could do it all for a piddling amount of money as long as I used cast bullets and saved that brass cartridge case. I carefully studied handgun accuracy and the effect of handguns on game. I took careful notes not only of results in the field but of every personal-defense shooting I could garner a reliable account of. Making a living with writing was about as likely as becoming a space captain, but I continued the practice of taking notes that began in my teenage years.

I had the opportunity to visit the Imperial War Museum in London and the Museum de Armee in Paris, whetting all the more an appetite for knowledge. I served as a peace officer for many years. Let me make a point concerning police work. When cops says they have seen something, we most often mean we arrived just after the incident ended. I may not have been an eyewitness to a .45 taking out an overcoat and two ribs, but I arrived just after it happened. There was a lot of action in the south. Our crimes and mysteries run from "Who drank the last of the iced tea?" and get a little rougher than "Who let the dog out?"

Every time I look in the mirror and see my scars I am reminded of the mayhem human beings are capable of. Some, like the robber who is frightened and panics and shoots his victim, use violence as a means to an end. Others love human pain and suffering. I am not turning to a dark note, but when I talk about the bad guys and that unfortunate and unreformable part of humanity, you must understand where I am coming from. Every man is like the moon. He has a dark side you do not always see, but it is there.

I became a writer and my hobby became my avocation. Without elaborating, among the first conversations I had with an editor was to call his publication and comment on an article I had read. I told the man there was no way it had happened the way the writer told it. I knew what happened when bullets met flesh and bone, be it man or beast, and I also knew exactly how accurate handguns were. The late Tom Ferguson was instrumental in launching my writing career. He told me to write gun articles the way I wrote police reports. Everything had to be verifiable, and if I did an experiment it had to be repeatable. I like to think the buying public has voted with their wallets, as I have published well over 1,200 articles, columns, and reviews, and I write for a number of reputable periodicals.

Over the years I have formed many opinions on handguns. I am not a doctrinaire on which handgun my students should use, and I certainly do not wish to produce a carbon copy of myself. I am at a pleasant stage in life in which my handguns do not have to work for a living. I own a number simply because I can. You should as well. I am a work in progress, and it seems that dying is a prerequisite for inclusion in a memoir. I am still kicking and I hope I will be for some time.

What follows is personal experience. I cannot honestly state that everything was learned the hard way, because handgunning is a pleasant thing. Experience is the most powerful learning tool. In this way new words criticize old words, and I have changed my mind on some subjects over the years. I think that no writer since the Apostle Paul should be confident in the permanent value of his words. Things and people change. I am not quite as obdurate as granite. I am capable of change. I hope the reader finds plain speaking and knowledge in these pages.

Introduction
A Brief History of the Handgun

NO ONE KNOWS WHEN THE first handgun was invented. There is specula-tion that handguns were carried and used by Chinese soldiers in the thir-teenth century. There is little doubt that by 1326 handguns were in common use. The first firearms were field pieces, large artillery pieces used in set piece battle.

The handgun was developed as a means of meeting a threat that was not foreseen. It could be carried ready to solve an unexpected problem. Early firearms used matchlocks, which simply meant that a burning match or string was pressed into the powder charge to fire the piece. The wheel lock was wonderfully compli-cated. Simpler locks led to less expensive firearms and greater use by rank-and-file soldiers. The flintlock proved to be the most enduring of the black powder firearms. This lock used a piece of flint held in place that ignited the powder charge when sparked against another piece of the lock. A finer grade of powder held in the pan was used to ignite the main powder charge. A great advance was the fulminate cap. This eliminated the need for the flint, offered more reliable ignition, and paved the way for the repeating handgun.

During the early years of the firearm, warfare changed but little. Siege engines were important and cold steel ruled the battlefield. The longbow and crossbow were less expensive and had a higher rate of fire than firearms. But the gradual development of more

This still life stirs our souls. A single-action revolver is carried in the Percival leather holster and a Colt pocket pistol lies nearby. *Percival Leather*

powerful and more accurate firearms eventually changed the face of battle. With handheld firearms able to penetrate armor, the mounted knight was no longer viable. Many types of defense were untenable against firearms. In most cases the long, heavy musket with its mounted bayonet carried the day, but not always by firepower. Hand-to-hand combat was the final arbitral of many battles.

The 1860 Colt Army Model was a great fighting handgun, well made and powerful. This one is offered by Dixie Gunworks and is a fine recreational handgun.

The handgun evolved into an important part of warfare and later, personal defense. A citizen facing brigands understood a new force in personal defense, the threat. Even a small single-shot pistol was an effective deterrent. No one wished to be shot, and which of the gang was willing to take the bullet? In the days before antibiotics a ball in the gut meant a slow and painful death. With a sword or rapier as the backup, the pistol became an important defense against the criminal element. The pistol also became a valued close-quarters weapon. Sailors

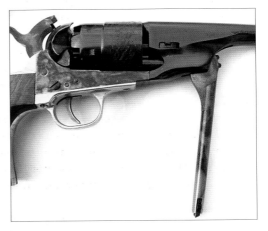

When the powder charge is placed in the cylinder the next step is to use the barrel-mounted ramrod to ram a ball home. While slow by modern standards, the Colt was a great advance over the flintlock pistol.

boarding enemy ships relied on cold steel and the cutlass but also a brace of pistols. The pistol in the hands of a mounted soldier allowed the cavalryman to extend his will beyond saber range.

Eventually handguns evolved that had sporting use. With the advent of rifled barrels this technology was applied to handguns. Dueling pistols appeared that were capable of extreme accuracy at moderate range. While invented with lethal intent, these were the first pistols accurate enough for practice to be meaningful. Pistol contests were undertaken and special firearms designed solely for gallery shooting were developed. The recreational value of firearms was well understood by the nineteenth century and became an important part of the firearms trade.

As an example, the Flobert cap, designed for inexpensive gallery shooting in an urban development, led to the wide spread use of rimfire ammunition and the wonderfully useful .22-caliber rimfire ammunition we have today.

Self-contained cartridges holding the powder charge, priming compound, and the projectile in one unit marked the rise of the modern firearm. These cartridges came into common use before the Civil War. Although their advantages were obvious, it was decades before they finally eclipsed the muzzle-loading firearm. The Colt cap-and-ball revolvers were in general use on the frontier well past 1880 and seem to have been a common staple of the shooting fraternity well into the twentieth century. Today, practically every type of firearm popular during the Western period is available as a reproduction, while the hoary old guns of the previous centuries seem to garner little interest.

Monumental developments occurred from 1860 to 1911. Practically every type of handgun design we use today was available in some form or the other. Break-top revolvers with double-action triggers were popular. Double-action swing-out cylinder revolvers

When the hammer is cocked, the percussion nipple is exposed. A fulminate cap is placed on this nipple to ignite the powder charge. When the handgun was new and in good tune this was a reliable system.

Both of these firearms are modern replicas of classic handguns. The Sharps rifle is offered by Taylor and Company. The .44-40-caliber revolver is a modern high-quality replica offered by Navy Arms.

The Smith & Wesson double-action–only top-break .38 was popular in the Old West. This revolver is in fine mechanical condition although well worn.

were developed soon afterward, as were the first self-loading handguns. Single-action and double-action and double-action–only handguns were readily available. Competition shooting flourished. So did hunting. In the American West the ever-present handgun was pressed into service as a defense against marauding wolves and coyote and even grizzly. The need for powerful reliable handguns was met by our manufacturers. Game was taken with the handgun by necessity and opportunity. Among the first recorded instances of sport hunting with the handgun comes from Buffalo Bill Cody. Cody and his cohorts took game at a gallop, firing from the back of their steed, often placing a bullet into the ear of a Buffalo. Cody was among the first exhibition shooters.

Throughout this period, the military use of the handgun was firmly established. The Colt cap-and-ball revolvers that were used during the Civil War were important historically as milestones in handgun development. These were the first reliable, powerful, and accurate repeating handguns. The old horse pistols had plenty of power, but the Colt gave six shots. Colt revolvers were more accurate at long-range than muskets. These handguns were responsible in part for the successful migration of settlers to the West. Before the advent of the Colt revolver, a single explorer or scout was at the mercy of aboriginal tribes. With the Colt, he could hold his own against superior numbers. Intelligently applied, the firepower of the Colt could become a problem for an entire infantry squad. During the Civil War it was common for cavalry soldiers to carry a brace of repeating revolvers, often as many as they could afford or obtain. These revolvers gave unprecedented firepower to a fast-moving trooper. These were among the first troops rightly called "shock troops."

Two classic handguns: The Navy Arms Deluxe SAA is a first-class single-action revolver capable of good accuracy. The H&R .38 is unusual as it has a long barrel. It handles and shoots well.

During the period immediately after the Civil War, there was a great deal of development in handguns. This was spurred by intense competition. A military contract could make a company wealthy and afford tremendous prestige worldwide. Smith & Wesson won one such contract with the Russian czar and produced a series of Russian model revolvers. These break-top single-action revolvers were prized for their accuracy and fast reloading. They were used not only by the Russians but the Japanese, facing each other during the Russo Japanese War. Some historians felt that the demands of the Russian contract had Smith & Wesson basically absent from the domestic market, but this is not strictly true. There were quite a few cowboys and Western lawmen who used the Smith & Wesson. The light break-top revolvers were especially popular as hideouts.

Colt developed the Single Action Army for use by our military, and the SAA was adopted in 1873. Some have stated that the SAA was dated even in 1873. It was a single-action, with a gate-loading mechanism that seemed quite slow compared to the break-top Smith & Wesson. The rod-ejecting mechanism was

In this fifteen-year-old photograph, the author's son uses a Uberti .45 to put a 255-grain bullet dead center of the target. The SAA handles well and offers plenty of short-range power.

used to laboriously eject each round one cartridge case at a time. But this mattered little in the scheme of things. The SAA was far faster to load than a cap-and-ball revolver. The solid frame of the Colt was rugged. The cartridge was among the first self-contained handgun cartridges. The .45 Colt Central Fire, as it was called, was reliable and accurate. A well-trained trooper could connect with an Indian War Pony at one hundred yards. More likely than not a solid hit with the .45 would put an opponent down for the count.

The Colt was so well respected that many soldiers carried the SAA long past the adoption of double-action revolvers and even after the advent of the 1911 self-loader. General George S. Patton carried his SAA throughout World War II and so did General Wainwright. The Colt was adopted by the majority of lawmen. The revolver was simple, rugged, and did what was needed. The SAA was carried by Wyatt Earp, Heck Thomas, and others. The SAA survived in use by many Western

A few steps in cartridge evolution, left to right: .22 Short cartridges, a 200-grain lead .38 bullet, two center-fire cartridges, and a .457-inch lead ball. All were in use at the turn of the last century, but the cap-and-ball revolver using lead balls is no longer in front line service.

lawmen far past the general adoption of more modern handguns by both large agencies and the military. Why? The Colt was proven. The Colt offered a fight-stopping cartridge and featured a light trigger release as well as a handle that fit most hands well. Notably, T. E. Lawrence, the legendary Lawrence of Arabia, used a Colt SAA during his archeological forays prior to World War I.

During the waning days of the Old West, in Europe a completely new type of handgun was being developed. Although there had been previous attempts at a self-loading handgun the smoky, dirty technology of black powder kept research on the type from proceeding. The invention of smokeless gunpowder in France changed the world. Previously, black powder residue gummed the action and would corrode the action practically overnight if the firearm was not cleaned. The widespread use of smokeless powder and jacketed bullets made a self-loading pistol possible. Once smokeless powder was available, research and development proceeded at a brisk pace.

By 1905, practically all modern handguns were either in widespread use or in development. These included self-loading pistols and single-action and double-action revolvers. Hunting, competition, and self-defense were in the province of these handguns. We should note that the rise of purebred target handguns simply meant that the pressure was off in some circles. Without the constant threat of war or warfare with the inhabitants of their own country, men could turn their attention to gamesmanship and other pursuits. We have never completely succeeded in beating our swords into plowshares, but competition shooting is a great game well worth your time and effort.

At this point, the history of the handgun has so many branches we are going to devote entire chapters to individual types. Safe to say, the handgun game was wild and wooly at the turn of the twentieth century, with many types of handguns competing for ascendancy over the other. High-velocity rounds with light bullets

The Smith & Wesson Perfected Model is among the finest top-break revolvers ever made. This design is a hinged-frame revolver that also incorporates a frame-mounted cylinder latch. It is a cross between the I-frame and the old break tops.

were offered, as were slow-moving heavy rounds. For the urban gentleman, self-loading pocket pistols were developed that remain popular to this day.

World War I was a great harrower, with death and destruction on an unprecedented scale. Due to the nature of trench warfare the handgun was very important. The study of the history of the handgun is a fascinating pursuit and absolutely essential for an understanding of the appeal of the pieces. I hope the following chapters will both enlighten readers and whet their appetite for further study in this fascinating game.

If these Webley revolvers could only speak. The top revolver is a World War II–era
version once used by Singapore police. The bottom Webley is a turn-of-the-century
.455 caliber.

The Webley revolver features simultaneous top ejection. All things considered, this is
not a bad revolver for personal defense if one can be found in good shape. The piece is
very interesting historically.

PART I

Different Types of Recreational Handguns

CHAPTER 1

Single-Action Revolvers

The Cowboy Way

BEFORE THE ADVENT OF THE revolver, there were attempts at creating repeating handguns. Most used double or triple barrels, some used a magazine, and some used various quick-loading devices. None were successful.

The first successful revolver was developed by Samuel Colt. The revolver is defined by a fixed barrel with a revolving cylinder behind the barrel. A lock mechanism behind the cylinder manipulates and rotates the cylinder. As the hammer is drawn to the rear and cocked against spring pressure, the hammer moves a piece called the hand. The hand catches a groove in the rear of the cylinder and rotates it into place. At this point the bolt or bolt stop rises and engages a notch in the cylinder of the revolver, locking it into place. The hammer remains cocked until the trigger is pressed, releasing the hammer. The hammer flies forward and strikes the primer or, in those days, the cap, igniting the powder charge and firing the revolver.

Each shot requires the same action be taken. The Colt revolver was a tremendous

This classic Colt is carried in a plain hard-working holster by Jim Lockwood of Legends in Leather. It doesn't get any better than this. Pure pride of ownership runs high with the Colt.

step forward in handgun technology, more so than anything invented in the previous five hundred years. Overnight we had a repeating handgun that gave a trained man the advantage over greater numbers. A man armed with two Colt pistols had more firepower than a brigand with a belt full of horse pistols.

The design of the Colt was ingenious. The revolving cylinder was drilled with chambers that held the powder charge. A removable nipple on the back of the cylinder provided ignition when charged with a fulminate cap. To make the Colt ready the powder was charged in each cylinder and a round ball placed over the charge. A ramrod under the barrel was used to seat each bullet home. Finally, the cylinder was topped with the firing caps. You were good to go with tremendous firepower. The Colt was first used in great number during the war with Mexico and became a staple of the Western movement. The Colt was copied, but none save perhaps the Remington equaled the quality. A trained man was now the equal of an untrained gang and could be a squad problem within fifty yards. Another advantage of the revolver was that the bore was rifled, giving it great accuracy. The Colt revolver was more accurate than the majority of muskets then in military use.

All was not perfect, however. There were gradual improvements in the lock mechanism or action to improve the ruggedness of the design. Power was also improved. The first Colt revolvers fired a .36-caliber ball. This ball expanded on contact with flesh-and-blood targets at close range. The effect, similar to a modern .38 Special hollow point, was often poor at ranges at which velocity had fallen and the round ball no longer expanded. This led to the development of .44-caliber revolvers. The Colt revolver was especially popular with the Texas Rangers. These men were on the point against not

Here is a trio of interesting modern single-action revolvers: starting at the top is a Navy Arms .44-40, then a Colt .22 Magnum, and a United States Firearms Rodeo. The Colt is out of production.

You have got to have something to carry the SAA in. This holster is by John Costanza, Western Star Leather. Few handguns are as well balanced as the SAA.

only Indian attacks but also Mexican bandits. The Colt saved the life of many a hard-bitten Ranger.

The revolver followed a gradual evolution to cartridge-firing examples. The revolvers we are going to discuss in this chapter are single-action revolvers. This simply means that the hammer must be cocked before each shot. The hammer is cocked, operating the action, and the cylinder is indexed for each shot. A press of the trigger drops the hammers. Since the trigger only accomplishes one action, the design is termed single-action. The double-action revolver uses the trigger to both cock and drop the hammer. If you consider the evolutionary aspects of the handgun, it might seem odd to some that the single-action remains popular. Not only is the type popular, new examples are introduced regularly. The advantages of the double-action revolver are obvious, including a swing-out cylinder and double-action trigger. For the single-action to survive, there must be something to it. In my opinion the single-action is the pure sporting handgun for today's handgunner. Nostalgia, emotional attachment, and a sense of history combine to make the single-action revolver a fascinating instrument. Whether you like to refer to the SAA as the Lawman's Gun or the Gun That Won the West, it is a tangible piece of history. It is the handgun carried by the original Indiana Jones—T. E. Lawrence.

The single-action revolver is our oldest repeating handgun. The Colt buried the pepperbox and other repeaters. It was so reliable, and eventually offered in so many frame sizes, nothing could compete save its imitators. Samuel Colt offered the revolver in pocket, belt, and horse pistol sizes of .31-, .36-, and .44-caliber. Today this basic relationship still exists between personal defense and service handguns. The later cartridge handguns are just fine for carrying on the belt when hiking or hunting in a hostile environment. The SAA, once the greatest warhorse in America, is now a recreational handgun.

The cap-and-ball black-powder revolvers are interesting, but the cartridge handguns are the most practical for daily use. Quite a few shooters continue to

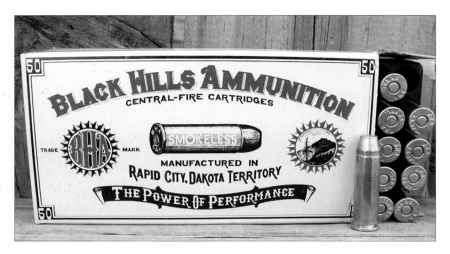

Even cartridge boxes are available that reflect the spirit of the Old West. Among our favorites is Black Hills. This is in inexpensive lead bullet load.

keep a single action revolver on hand for home defense use. My best recommendations for modern gear aside, if you are cognizant with the reality of manipulating a single-action handgun under stress, then the SAA may not be an ideal choice but it is acceptable. I would not wish to encounter an accomplished single-action shooter on a dark night. Those who shoot Cowboy Action matches are very, very good at what they do and doubtless better shots overall than the majority of shooters in the Old West. Thousands of folks enjoy this competition and enjoy burning gunpowder in the single action. The tactical hypochondriac with his high-capacity 9mm and four spare magazines may laugh, but the joke could be on him when his 9mm doesn't do the business! A quality self-loader chambered for the .45 ACP is a better personal-defense handgun in trained hands and a quality double-action revolver in .44 Magnum is quite a hunting handgun. But in the end the handgun is simply a projectile launcher, isn't it? The man or woman behind the sights is what matters.

The single-action revolver is ponderously slow to load. The hammer is placed at half-cock and the loading gate opened. Cartridges are loaded one at a time as the cylinder is indexed. To unload, the reverse is undertaken, with each cartridge punched out by the ejector rod. Some love this manipulation as much as firing; others tire of it in one fell swoop. And that's okay. That is why there are different types of handguns. But one of my acquaintances, a seasoned trail lawyer, keeps a Colt SAA .45 for home defense. He states that he knows it is safe at a glance and that cocking the hammer is a deliberate action not likely to be fumbled or misinterpreted. Like all experienced single-action shooters, he keeps the revolver loaded with only five rounds.

A drawback with the single-action Colt design is that the firing pin would rest upon the primer of the chambered cartridge if the hammer were lowered on the

All single-actions on the frontier were not Colts. This is Smith & Wesson's break-top revolver. The leather is by Percival. *Percival Leather*

loaded cylinder. So we keep this cylinder empty. This is the five-beans-under-the-wheel rule. The rule is simple to apply. Load one cartridge, skip a cylinder; load four, cock the hammer and lower it. You will be on the empty cylinder. This simple rule will save lots of hardship. Properly holstered, a single-action with the hammer down on an empty chamber is well suited to motorcycle riding, horseback riding, and any number of head-over-heels pursuits. The SAA is well balanced and the grip fits most hands well. The plow-handled shape of the SAA is comfortable even when firing heavy loads. Despite the long hammer fall of the SAA, accuracy is often excellent.

The SAA Army in modern times has been copied by many makers, primarily Uberti of Italy and a few other European makers. These include SIG SAUER and Arminius. The quality of these revolvers varies drastically. I would avoid the brass-frame revolvers. Single-action revolvers use variations on the single-action theme, including the transfer bar type we will discuss at a later date. The Colt, when cocked, clicks as the cylinder is indexed. Legend has it these clicks spell C-O-L-T. A Colt man has ears to hear, but the legendary clicks fall on deaf ears to the heathen.

The single-action may be divided into three main types: the foreign-produced single-action revolvers, the American SAA types, and the Ruger. The Uberti is by far the most common of the foreign revolvers. These handguns range from inexpensively made versions I cannot recommend to excellent examples of the gunmaker's art. As an example, the Navy Arms Deluxe, sometimes cataloged as the Gunfighter, is an Uberti imported by Navy Arms. This revolver features a nickel silver grip frame and excellent attention to detail. The action contains the same W. C. Wolff premium gun springs we often use to tune up Uberti revolvers. This revolver has given excellent service and surprising accuracy. I wanted one in 4 3/4-inch barrel length and .45 Colt. I settled for a .44-40 and 5 1/2-inch length, or a wait of several months would have been entailed. Happily, the choice was a good one.

The .44-40 is a rather underrated cartridge. I have hand loaded it a great deal and find the .44-40 useful, accurate, and powerful. This example of the Uberti is a far cry from the Uberti revolvers I used during the 1970s. The company has discovered that we are willing to pay for quality. Fit and finish are excellent and the Navy Arms product is a desirable handgun. Other than for investment purposes I see no real reason to purchase a Colt over the Navy Arms product. There are cautions with all handguns, but if you purchase the Navy Arms revolver or the Beretta Stampede you should have a long-lived revolver, given periodic maintenance. There are examples of the Uberti type such as the Beretta—Beretta now owns Uberti—that offer the transfer bar ignition while retaining the original half-cock notch. This is a great improvement in safety. After examining the type, however, I still recommend that we carry only five beans under the wheel with the transfer-bar-equipped single-action revolver.

The American-made United States Firearms revolvers are identical in most regards to the Colt SAA. The Colt is now an expensive custom shop item, and the USFA is a dependable alterative. Most writers agree that the USFA is overall superior to the Colt as far as accuracy and workmanship are concerned. This is

This is a special edition from Sturm Ruger. The bird's-head grip, 4 3/4-inch barrel and .32 H&R Magnum chambering make for an exciting revolver.

A single-action revolver is being loaded. The hammer is at half cock and the loading gate is open. The chamber is an index to the loading port.

In this photograph a single-action revolver is cocked and ready to fire. All that is required to drop the hammer is that the trigger be pressed.

a bold claim that is difficult to dispute. The fit and finish of USFA revolvers are impeccable. The revolver features a good tight barrel and cylinder gap that affords good accuracy potential. My example has proven reliable, accurate, and free of binding. I would move this revolver past the recreational shooting limits of the Uberti into the state at which you may rely upon the handgun for defense use against man or beast. Yet they are true to the style of the SAA.

When studying the single-action revolver, I have reached definite conclusions as to the historical of these handguns. Curiously, period photographs and literature confirm that the Colt was carried long after the introduction of the double-action revolver and the 1911 .45 pistol. By the 1930s, the .44 Special double-action revolver was popular, and those who could afford it adopted the

.357 Magnum after 1935. But the SAA survived in the hands of not only weather-beaten older lawmen but younger men as well. I think that the well shaped handle of the SAA had a lot to do with that. Even with the heaviest .45 Colt loadings the handgun was controllable and comfortable to fire. A seasoned handgunner could use recoil to his advantage. The single-action's barrel rose in recoil, dipping the hammer down. The shooter's thumb then grasped the hammer, cocking it on the rebound. Thus, fast shooting and good repeat hits are possible.

The single-action offered a crisp single-action trigger press. The double-action revolver required more trigger finger work, and the grip frame was not nearly as comfortable. I noted that these men often moved to the 1911 .45 auto and skipped the double-action revolver altogether, probably because the advantages of the 1911, including two additional shots, were too great to ignore. The 1911 automatic pistol also featured a grip frame that fit just about anyone's hand well and a single-action trigger compression. Still, the 1911 was not universally praised even within the services.

The Ruger differs in loading sequence from other single-action types. The loading gate may be opened with the hammer fully down.

A few die-hards used the SAA .45 and nothing else. General George S. Patton took his toll of Mexican bandits when armed with the SAA .45. He dropped these dangerous bandits and then threw them across the hood of his touring car. Patton was an Olympic shooting champion and a deadly shot with the pistol. In common with Douglas MacArthur, Patton found himself in a situation in Mexico in which he fired his Colt .45 empty. Obviously both lived to tell the tale and neither, as far as I am aware, adopted the 1911 after this experience. Patton solved his dilemma by beginning to carry two .45-caliber revolvers. When you see a photograph of a cowboy, soldier, or gunfighter wearing two pistols—and few actually did except in times of war—it was not in order to use a handgun in each hand. Rather, the idea was to be able to stay in action by drawing the backup.

Wild Bill Hickock carried a pair of beautifully balanced Colt Navy .36-caliber pistols long past the SAA era for much the same reason, but Hickock was among the few gunfighters able to fire with either hand as well as the other. Patton later adopted the .357 Magnum as one of his belt guns, but the Colt SAA survived and more soldiers than General Patton carried the old gun into battle. Primarily these were officers of the old school.

Today the single-action revolver is best suited for recreational shooting. As long as Cowboy Action Shooting is around, there will be a market for single-action revolvers of the original type. There are few handguns that are as great a joy to manipulate and load and fire. I would hate to give up my single-action revolvers. They are not high on the list for personal defense, but then they are great handguns with a ferocious pedigree.

RUGER SINGLE-ACTION REVOLVERS

The Ruger Blackhawk and Super Blackhawk revolvers are in a class by themselves. The Ruger features single-action styling, but the Ruger is much

This is the Ruger Montado, a special edition for mounted events in cowboy action shooting. Note the special grip and short barrel as well as the custom hammer.

stronger than any SAA. The Ruger is generally regarded as the strongest handgun ever produced. The original Blackhawk was introduced in the mid-1950s. The Colt Single Action Army was out of production and the fast draw sport was just sweeping the country. Celebrities such as Johnny Cash and Sammy Davis Jr. (a master of the fast draw) became fans.

Ruger saw a market for a revolver durable enough to withstand the rigors of fast-draw competition. The revolver is cocked vigorously and the action worked by fanning or holding the trigger back and sweeping the heel of the weak hand across the hammer. Since most shooting is done with blanks against a timer, this type of handling is okay as far as safety goes, but is hard on the handgun. Bill Ruger decided to produce a modern version of the single-action that would stand up to this handling and also to Magnum ammunition. He succeeded brilliantly.

The original .357 Magnum Blackhawk featured a ramp front post and fully adjustable rear sights. The revolver was quickly adopted by hunters and outdoorsmen, as well as those who treasured the single-action revolver. The sights are models for accuracy. By using coil wire rather than leaf springs, the action was extremely durable. The original .357 Magnum version was later upgraded to a .44

The SAA is compact for its caliber. At top is a double-action .357 Magnum revolver and at the bottom a double-action .38 Hand Ejector. The USFA .45, center, is compact for its power.

Magnum and finally the Super Blackhawk with an unfluted cylinder and Dragoon-style grip frame. Today, the .357, .41, and .44 Magnum Ruger revolvers are popular, and so is the .45 Colt chambering. The Super Blackhawk has taken game all over the world in the hands of skilled hunters. The accuracy of the type at long range is well known.

Not surprisingly with such a well distributed handgun, the Ruger Blackhawk has figured into quite a few defensive situations. I am aware of one such incident in which a hiker defended himself against a bear. A single .357 Magnum did the business. In another incident a park ranger ran across two dangerous wanted felons. One made a break for a long gun; the other grabbed a pistol. The crusty old outdoorsmen stopped both with his .44 Magnum Ruger Super Blackhawk. My particular example has proven almost incredibly accurate with the Black Hills 300-grain heavyweight load. The Super Blackhawk gives the shooter great confidence.

Among the advantages of the present Ruger revolver is the transfer bar ignition system. Although it was well known on the frontier that the single-action revolver should be carried with only five rounds, there is always someone who does not get the message. There were several incidents in which shooters suffered an accident with single-action revolvers.

Ruger redesigned his single-action revolver with the transfer bar system also used in the Ruger Security Six double-action revolver. With this system, the firing pin is located in the frame. There is a bar in the receiver that is between the hammer and the firing pin. When at rest, the hammer cannot reach the firing pin. There is no chance of an accidental discharge. When the hammer is fully cocked the cocking action also brings the transfer bar upwards. When the hammer falls, it strikes the transfer bar and the transfer bar strikes the firing pin. This is by far the safer system. The

It is relatively simple to maintain a single-action revolver. The cylinder is removed by removing the base bin. This does not affect the revolver's timing.

Ruger loading sequence is also changed. When the loading gate is opened, the cylinder is loaded and indexed without any need to bring the hammer to half cock. While some of us still adopt the five beans under the wheel carry with the modern Ruger, the Ruger is safe to carry fully loaded with six rounds.

Ruger also produces a single-action fixed-sight revolver known as the Vaquero. There are certain special editions such as the Montado (Mounted Cowboy) that rival the single-actions offered by custom pistol smiths. These revolvers do not quite have the same feel and balance as the SAA, but they are rugged and will take the pounding of thousands of rounds of ammunition without fail.

There are some who feel that the single-action is so outdated that anyone contemplating using the thumb buster for personal defense had best have their spiritual and temporal affairs in order. To others, the single-action revolver is an essential expression of their character, sacred to some and profane to others. If you feel the single-action is a marvelous relic of a bygone day, file this chapter under fun at the range or a theoretical exercise. There are better handguns for personal defense and hunting, but none more powerful or more reliable. I have lost count of the good guys and girls who have defended themselves with the single-action revolver.

The first felon I took at gunpoint was held for the police on the point of a Colt single-action revolver. If you shoot Cowboy Action or hunt with a single-action there is a lot of familiarity there. The single-action demands effort in loading and unloading. The fastest reload I have ever seen was eighteen seconds, and this is ponderously slow. This being said, the single-action is far from done in serving in its most vital role. The Old West lives in the hearts and minds of those who use the single-action revolver. While many wonder why one would shoot such a relic, we can only reply, "Because we can."

CHAPTER 2

Trigger-Cocking Revolvers

TRIGGER-COCKING REVOLVERS OR DOUBLE-ACTION REVOLVERS were invented almost immediately after the Colt revolver was introduced. The pepperbox was in some ways a double-action–only revolver, but the pepperbox was never reliable or accurate. The Allen and Thurber pepperbox used a double-action trigger to move the cylinder in rotation, and the hammer dropped and fired each cylinder in turn. There were also single-action pepperbox handguns, and the modern COP .357 was arguably the last pepperbox.

Trigger cocking or double action means that a single press of the trigger both cocks and fires the revolver. Since the trigger serves two functions, the term "double action" is as accurate as the term "trigger cocking." With most double-action revolvers there is also a single-action notch that allows the hammer to be cocked for a deliberate shot. Concealed hammer revolvers normally do not use a single-action notch. They are double-action–only revolvers. Service revolvers such as the Adams and Deane were delivered with double-action–only triggers. The British in particular felt that

The revolver will last thousands of rounds and give good service. This is a stainless-steel Smith & Wesson Model 66 .357 Magnum revolver. It has perhaps 10,000 rounds on the frame.

This is a rare bird: a Colt Official Police in .22 caliber. Primarily intended as a trainer, this is among the most accurate .22-caliber revolvers ever produced.

all combat revolvers should be delivered with a double-action–only trigger, and there is some truth in this.

Today we associate double-action triggers with swing-out cylinder revolvers, but in the early days of revolver use there were many double-action revolvers that were basically single-action types with a double-action mechanism. They loaded in the same manner as single-action revolvers. Possibly the last of these was the Colt Frontier Double Action, an adaptation of the SAA to a double-action trigger mechanism. Such lash ups are not always workable, but this handgun seemed to have a good reputation. Smith & Wesson relied primarily upon break-top action revolvers until the late 1890s, and quite a few of these revolvers were offered with a double-action trigger.

The lighter .32- and .38-caliber double-action Smith & Wesson revolvers were particularly popular. The advantage of the double-action trigger was in fast combat shooting at close range. Since the handgun is primarily carried for defense against an unforeseen threat, the ability to draw and fire the handgun quickly without cocking a hammer was deemed important.

Revolvers come in all shapes and sizes but follow a certain pattern. Both of these are four-inch-barrel Smith & Wesson revolvers with the round-butt grip frame. The upper revolver is a .44 Special, the bottom, a .32 Smith & Wesson Long.

Once Colt pioneered the solid-frame swing-out cylinder revolver, the die was cast. All service revolvers adopted after 1892 would be swing-out cylinder designs with double-action triggers almost without exception. The Smith & Wesson break tops survived for a time and the British Webley remained in service throughout World War II, but the Smith & Wesson revolver was immensely popular. The Colt and the Smith went head to head in competition, but today Colt no longer competes in the revolver field. This is sad because some of the greatest revolvers of all time wore the Colt pony on their side.

The first double-action revolvers in general use were more fragile than the revolvers we have today. The Colt Model of 1892 was adopted by the U.S. Army in 1892. While upgraded to an extent with different versions the Colt .38 was a failure. Never a rugged design, the cartridge that the '92 chambered is terribly underpowered. When pressed into service in the Philippines, the .38 failed miserably. There are accounts of Moro warriors taking six and seven or even more rounds from the .38 without effect. The .45 caliber SAA revolvers were rushed to the front as a

The Smith & Wesson Model 27 is perhaps the most accurate .357 Magnum revolver ever produced. This one is the very desirable three-and-one-half-inch barrel version.

The Colt Official Police double-action revolver is a well balanced and smooth revolver with an impeccable pedigree. This one is chambered for the .22 Long Rifle cartridge.

stop gap. Eventually both Colt and Smith & Wesson produced quality swing-out cylinder double-action revolvers equal to the task. The big-frame Smith & Wesson and the Colt New Service chambered serious fight-stopping cartridges. While they were replaced by a big-bore autoloader in military use, the big-bore double-action revolver remained an important revolver in police circles and in civilian hands.

The last big hurrah for the double-action revolver was World War I. Thousands of Colt and Smith & Wesson revolvers were cambered for the .45 ACP cartridge and shipped to Europe. There were not enough 1911 automatics to go around, and the revolvers made it possible to arm troops with a sidearm. Historians have stated that 72 percent of U.S. troops were armed with handguns by the end of the war. Big-bore revolvers, already in production for the British in .455 caliber, filled a much needed gap in supply when produced in versions chambered for the American .45 ACP cartridge. These revolvers used a special half-moon clip to allow chambering the rimless .45 automatic pistol cartridge.

Speaking of the British, the British Webley is well worth our attention. The Webley served from 1887 until 1963 in various Marks and modifications. The Webley features a top break or hinged frame. While not particularly strong by modern standards, the action was strong enough for the modest pressure of the cartridges used in these revolvers. Most of the Marks were introduced prior to World War I, with the Mark VI among the most widely used in combat during that war. The Webley was a big, rugged robust design that chambered a big-bore cartridge with proven stopping power. The .455 Webley is a rather sedate round, throwing a 265-grain lead bullet at 620 feet per second, but the .455 Webley enjoyed a good reputation.

The British adopted a much lighter .38-caliber break-top revolver after World War I. They took the unusual step of adopting the American .38 Smith & Wesson cartridge but with a special loading using a 200-grain bullet. Many Webley revolvers were used after the adoption of the lighter cartridge, and the similar Enfield revolver was also adopted, with the Enfield being used more widely. The Enfield was a true combat revolver with a spurless hammer and double-action–only trigger. While quite different from our own double-action revolvers, the Webley designs were important combat revolvers. They were not target guns or small-game revolvers by any means. They served a real purpose for the British Army.

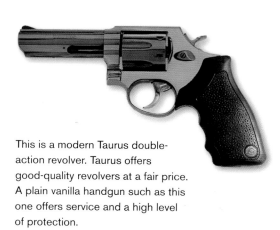

This is a modern Taurus double-action revolver. Taurus offers good-quality revolvers at a fair price. A plain vanilla handgun such as this one offers service and a high level of protection.

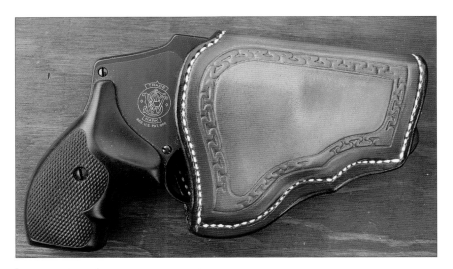

A snub .38 is compact. This one is carried in a Jeffrey Custom Leather holster. It is compact and brilliantly fast into action.

A drawback of the break-top revolvers, both Webley and Smith & Wesson, was that only a relatively short cartridge case could be used. The revolvers did not have sufficient leverage in the design to use a long cartridge case. This doomed the evolution of the design.

Around the turn of the previous century several revolvers were developed that went on to become among the most widely distributed handguns of all time. The big-frame handguns were popular with men who really needed a handgun, but the mid-frame or .38-caliber handguns were popular with those who may need a handgun. The handgun was carried as a convenience or just in case. Smith & Wesson's Hand Ejector was introduced in 1899, originally chambered for the anemic .38 Colt cartridge. The .38 Colt, or .38 Long Colt as it is sometimes called, propelled a 152-grain bullet at about 750 feet per second. Smith & Wesson introduced the .38 Special in 1902. With a heavier 158-grain bullet and velocity increased to a nominal 850 feet per second, the cartridge was superior to the .38 Colt. The Hand Ejector was also a more durable design than the Colt 1902.

Smith & Wesson improved the revolver in increments and eventually renamed the Hand Ejector, calling it the Military and Police. In 1958, the Military and Police became the Model Ten. The best estimate is that some six million have been manufactured. At one time well over three-quarters of the police departments in the United States carried the Model Ten. Others carried a variant such as the Combat Magnum. A few agencies carried the Colt, but by the 1980s Smith & Wesson had consolidated their lead into dominance in police sales. The Smith & Wesson was chambered primarily in .38 Special, but there were versions in .32–20

WCF, .38 Smith & Wesson, and even 9mm Luger. A few .22-caliber Military and Police handguns were produced.

During World War II the United States purchased more than one million for military use. Some were used by sailors and criminal investigation (CID) personnel, and many others were issued to guards at military installations. More than half a million were supplied to the United Kingdom during the war. These were chambered for the .38/200, a special variant of the .38 Smith & Wesson, a short .38, using a 200-grain bullet. The Military and Police revolver was amazingly versatile. The revolver was supplied with both round and square butt handles and two-, three-, four-, five-, and six-inch barrels. The Model 12 was an air-weight or aluminum-frame version that was popular with professionals during the 1960s to 1990s.

The stretch of the design was seen clearly in later developments. By adding a rib to the barrel and fitting adjustable sights, Smith & Wesson produced first-class target pistols. The Combat Masterpiece was the four-inch version; the six-inch version was the K 38. Even more impressive was the Combat Magnum. The Combat Magnum is simply a target sighted .38 Special revolver with the cylinder

There are configurations of the revolver suited to every need. Our friend B. K. is firing a Taurus Judge in .45/.410, her bedroom defender.

This young student had never fired a firearm before attending the author's classes. He was broken in with a Colt .22 manufactured in 1936. No wonder he is smiling.

elongated to enable the revolver to chamber the powerful .357 Magnum cartridge. Naturally, heat treating and metallurgy played a part.

The four-inch barrel Combat Magnum was used by many police agencies. While some of them loaded the revolver with .38 Special loads—often the hot +P or +P+ versions—some used the full-power Magnum. (The .357 Magnum is simply a .38 Special lengthened one-tenth of an inch and loaded to nearly twice the pressure of the .38 Special.) The K 38, a six-inch barrel .38 Special target-grade revolver, was among the greatest match-winning revolvers of all time.

Back to the N-frame revolvers: In the time between the wars the police needed more powerful handguns to deal with our new mechanized bandits. The .38 Special was a poor man stopper with standard loads. The .44 Special and the .45 Colt lobbed big slow-moving bullets that stopped felons with finality, but they were poor choices against sheet metal. The .38–44 was developed. This is simply a hot-loaded .38 Special, as far as the cartridge goes, but the revolver was a heavy-frame Smith & Wesson chambered for the .38 Special cartridge. This combination achieved 1,100 feet per second with factory loads, and with heavy handloads 1930s experimenters reached 1,300 feet per second with the 158-grain bullet. A cast-lead hollow point at this velocity had great penetration on sheet metal and good effect on felons. Smith & Wesson developed the .357 Magnum revolver as a result of experiments with the .38–44. This is among the single most influential revolvers of all time. Offered in a premium package the .357 Magnum offered unprecedented power, accuracy, and quality. The revolver came with a heavy price tag. Sales were not substantial, but the prestige of the new Magnum gave Smith & Wesson a lead in the industry that Colt never challenged again.

The Model 27 is a superbly crafted revolver that will challenge the skill of any shooter. I have never successfully qualified the accuracy of this handgun, but it's safe to say that with carefully tailored handloads the revolver will group five shots into two inches at fifty yards. This is about twice as accurate as the most accurate current production autoloaders, save for a few. The Model 27 is still treasured by some of us, but it is also evident that the revolver became too expensive to manufacture and there was too little demand for the type. The Model 27 was discontinued some years ago. The next step was the mighty .44 Magnum revolver. The N-frame .44 Special was given much the same treatment that the .38 was given, and a powerful and accurate handgun was the result.

There are the classic hideout and personal-defense revolvers. At top is a nickel-plated Colt Detective Special. The lower piece is a Smith & Wesson Chief's Special, stainless steel, both in .38 Special.

Even today, with the advent of ever more powerful cartridges, the .44 Magnum remains the single most powerful cartridge that most of us are able to handle comfortably, and then only those willing to put great amounts of practice in may claim to have truly mastered this cartridge. Without the development of these cartridges, handgun hunting would have been limited to modest size game and equally modest ranges.

After World War II, Smith & Wesson did not set on its laurels, but before the Combat Magnum the company introduced an even more popular revolver. For some years it had produced light six-shot .32s and a five-shot .38 using the short .38 Smith & Wesson cartridge. Smith took the bold step of strengthening the I-frame revolver, lengthening the cylinder, and producing a five-shot .38 Special hideout revolver. Introduced at a chief of police convention in 1949, the revolver was named the Chief's Special. The revolver was offered in round and square butt configuration, eventually in both steel and aluminum frame, and with two- and three-inch barrels. Even target-sighted handguns were introduced, although they are rare. Today Chief's Special variants are available in .32 H&R Magnum, .38 Special, and .357 Magnum. They are available in concealed-hammer variants and a number of handguns in the Classic Series.

Colt introduced the Army Special that became the Colt Official Police to compete with the Smith & Wesson Military and Police around the turn of the

These are great shooting revolvers. The upper revolver is a special version originally intended for the New York City Police Department, a three-inch heavy barrel Chief's Special. The lower handgun is an Airweight Military and Police revolver, the Model 12.

previous century. Colt had the jump on Smith & Wesson when Colt introduced a swing-out cylinder double-action first-shot revolver in 1889. This revolver led to the disappointing Model 1892, but the later Army Special was a great revolver. It is interesting to note that the Colt was offered on a .41 frame and was sometimes chambered for the .41 Long Colt. The .41-caliber Colt actually used a .384-inch-diameter bullet and at its low velocity had little to recommend it over the .38 Special. The primary chambering for this revolver was the .38 Special.

Without any army contracts on the horizon, Colt reacted to Smith & Wesson's changes. Smiths, as we affectionately call them, decided to change the name of the Hand Ejector to Military and Police. The Army Special became Colt's Official Police. The Colt Official Police was a popular revolver that was used by discerning officers world wide. The Colt was often given the nod for smoothness and accuracy while the Smith & Wesson was thought to have the advantage in longevity. The Colt Official Police was the basis for the development of the popular Colt Python revolver. The Official Police proved to be a good revolver, but it was eventually eclipsed by the Smith & Wesson revolvers. While the Colt Official Police was not manufactured in the millions as the Smith & Wesson Military and Police has been, and it is no longer in production, three hundred thousand revolvers is nothing to sneeze at.

Colt's small-frame six-shot revolvers were lighter than the Smith & Wesson and enjoyed a great deal of popularity with those who did not like the drag of a heavy revolver on the belt. The Police Positive was chambered in the lighter .32 and .38 calibers, but the popular Police Positive Special was chambered for the powerful .38 Special cartridge. Colt created a true classic in 1926 with the introduction of the popular streamlined two-inch barrel Detective Special. The Detective Special is so smooth and accurate it may be fired as accurately as most four-inch barrel service pistols. The Detective Special is a wonderful defense revolver, possessed of many good features. The Chief's Special outsold the Colt primarily because it was smaller, lighter, and less expensive. The Colt was a class act that has not been followed.

As we deal with the history of the trigger-cocking revolver you may easily see that the great revolvers of the previous century were important handguns in the personal-defense scene. The Magnum revolvers became important on the hunting scene. Previously, handguns were carried primarily as backup to finish off game. Now, with the advent of the Magnum revolvers, a hunter could rely on the Magnum to take game cleanly well past one hundred yards. This was an important step in the evolution of firearms. By the same token we had on hand all of the important innovations in concealed-carry revolvers by 1955. These innovations included the adoption of high-quality aircraft grade aluminum for use in the manufacture of lightweight-frame revolvers. The Magnums and some of the autoloaders are more interesting to own and shoot, but I think that the words of the late Tom Ferguson are important at this point. Tom was a longtime peace officer of great experience. Unlike many writers, Tom had real-world experience in the street and he was a

Big, heavy, and with quite a character, the Smith & Wesson .44 Magnum revolver is a lot of revolver. Popular for hunting and simply for pride of ownership, the Models 29 and 629 are great revolvers.

seasoned firearms expert. Tom called the Smith & Wesson Military and Police .38 Special the "gunfighter's gun of the twentieth century." The plain vanilla four-inch barrel .38 probably spoke in favor of more harness cops than all of the rest of the handguns in general use put together.

A final point: These great handguns of the past were well made of good material. The Smith & Wesson Model 27, the Model 29 .44 Magnum, and the Combat Magnum are available on the used gun market. The Colt Official Police, the Detective Special, and the Python are also available. They are great handguns, but do not go to the gun show cash in hand unless you are qualified to inspect and determine the condition of each example. If you wish to own a good shooting revolver, Smith & Wesson offers the same models or equivalents in the Classic line. These handguns feature transfer bar ignition that among other advantages seem to handle heavy loads in a superior manner. The cylinder and throat dimensions of the modern Smith & Wesson revolvers make for more consistent accuracy. CNC machinery is very consistent. Do not be disappointed if you cannot find an original, as the new revolvers are practical and well made of good material. Just the same, there is something in steel that has been around a few decades.

CHAPTER 3

Mauser to Browning: The First Self-Loaders

IN 1883, HIRAM MAXIM INVENTED the first Maxim machine gun. At the same time, others were attempting to use the firing gas of a firearm to work the action. John Moses Browning converted a Winchester lever-action rifle to fully automatic fire by installing a gas trap at the muzzle, along with other modifications. The gas trap captured the gas produced on firing and redirected gas pressure to operate the action. Maxim's toggle lock proved useful in the appropriate application for handguns.

Hugo Borchardt took the unique knee-joint toggle-locking action of the Maxim machine gun and applied it to a self-loading pistol. Along the way, he designed a powerful cartridge, the 7.63x25mm that was used later in the Mauser M96. The Borchardt pistol was large, heavy, and best suited for use with the supplied shoulder stock. Just the same, it was a breakthrough design with many good features. Georg Luger took the design, downsized it, and created the Luger pistol. Before Luger perfected his handgun, Paul Mauser's factory was turning out the C96 Mauser. The

The Mauser HSc has an art deco look that makes it endearing to collectors. This example is a modern Interarms import in .380 ACP.

Feedrele brothers, Fidel, Freidrick, and Josef were contracted to design and perfect this handgun. They did so, and by 1897 the Mauser C 96 was in production.

The C96 was often called the Broomhandle Mauser, although the Finns called it the Ukko or Old Man Mauser. The Broomhandle earned its name from its unusual appearance. The magazine is located in front of the trigger guard with the handle protruding like a broom handle under the receiver. The Broomhandle pistol looks ungainly but when held in the hand the pistol is actually quite well balanced.

The C96 used an oscillating wedge to lock and unlock the action, making it among the first full-power locked-breech handguns. The Mauser featured a bolt that recoils to the rear and a well designed safety that resembled a rifle safety in operation. The Mauser was a reliable pistol. Even today, the reputation of the Mauser is solid. The Mauser is more reliable than the German Luger, but the Luger was preferred because the Luger was lighter and handier. The Mauser earned a tremendous reputation in its day. The Mauser was first used in the Boer War, often with stunning effect. Although the pistol cartridge it chambered was a small caliber (.30), the Broomhandle round was among the highest velocity pistol cartridges ever fielded, reaching over 1,400 feet per second. Period authorities agree that the cartridge was a good stopper if it hit bone, and that its penetration against web gear was excellent.

The Mauser is a large pistol. It is 12 inches overall, with a 5.5-inch barrel and a weight of forty-three ounces. Just the same, the balance is good and the Mauser is often accurate. As a side note, the Mauser was once popular on the West Coast as a shark-killing gun for fishermen. Most pistols would not penetrate deeply enough in water to kill a marauding shark. High-power rifles would sometimes be used but

The German Luger is a pure joy to use and fire. This is a commercial version in .30 Luger. It has never stuttered with Fiocchi ammunition.

The Walther P38 is among the most influential handguns of all time. This war-time example is both reliable and accurate, although it's rather worn.

The Radom 9mm is a very interesting pistol. This example is one of the rougher late-production versions, as you may note by an absence of the early take-down lever. The pistol is both accurate and reliable. At some point an earlier owner, no doubt proud of his pistol, had this one nickel plated, ruining the collector value.

often the bullet would tear itself to pieces in water. Water is hard on bullets. The hard-jacketed 86-grain Mauser bullet was ideal. When dealing with sharks at close range, the Mauser was a handgun of choice. The Mauser was expensive when new and remained a substitute standard for the German Army, never a first-line pistol.

During World War I, the famous Red 9 pistols were produced. These were delivered in 9mm Luger caliber with a big red 9 engraved in the grips to make certain that the correct ammunition was loaded in these pistols. About 300,000 Mauser pistols were used by Germany during the first World War, including 136,000 Red 9 variants. The Mauser was produced until 1936 in various versions, including fully automatic pistols with detachable magazines. The pistol has a well deserved reputation for reliability and ruggedness.

The Luger was first offered in a special short .30 cartridge known as the .30 Luger. This loading propels an 86-grain bullet at about 1,200 feet per second. (Like the Mauser round, the Luger cartridge is available in a high-quality loading from Fiocchi USA.) Both the Mauser and the Luger featured a barrel and mechanism exposed to the elements. This was common in the day. The Luger action is strong. It is estimated that the barrel would blow before the action. The trigger feels odd to a modern shooter, but the Luger trigger is controllable and the pistol is often

The Colt 1911 is a wonderful pistol on all counts, still the greatest combat pistol ever produced. This modern version wears Adams and Adams engraving custom grips. It is both a showpiece and a hardy defender.

very accurate. The Luger never enjoyed a great reputation for reliability. There are many factors, including tired recoil springs and worn-out magazines. At its best, with new springs and a good Triple K magazine, the Luger is dependent upon properly loaded ammunition. The original loadings included a 124-grain bullet at about 1,200 feet per second and various 116-grain loads at even higher velocity.

I have clocked domestic 9mm 124-grain loads at less than 1,000 feet per second in the early 1980s. The Luger would not function well with loads of less than optimum power. While it is often advisable to use light loads with older handguns, the Luger is a strong firearm. The 9mm NATO-type loads—124 grains at more than 1,200 feet per second—usually function perfectly in the old war dog. Just the same, the Luger must be kept clean and lubricated for good function.

It is interesting to note that the German Luger was one of the first self-loading handguns the U.S. Army experimented with. The Army ordered some 1,000 .30-caliber versions the first of the twentieth century, and later ordered a smaller quantity in 9mm Luger. The Army appears to have been impressed with the workmanship of the Luger, with the self-loading firearm in general and with the accuracy potential of the piece. But reliability was far from impressive. The effect of the .30 Luger on animals was poor. For foraging and personal defense the Luger received a poor grade. John Moses Browning was developing his semiautomatic pistols at the same time, but Browning followed a different path.

Browning's designs were so influential that virtually every semi-automatic pistol since has incorporated his principles into the design. One of the great advances made by Browning was the enclosed slide. Few realize how important the enclosed slide is today. Practically every successful semi-automatic pistol in the world, including the Glock, SIG, Colt, and H and K uses a slide that encloses the firing pin and barrel and also keeps the recoil spring hidden as well as preventing debris from falling into the receiver. Browning perfected the slide and also the locked-breech action. In the locked-breech action the barrel and slide remain locked together in recoil. The barrel and slide recoil together and remain locked together until the bullet exits the barrel.

At this point pressure from firing abates and the barrel and slide are separated. The slide recoils to the rear and the spent case is ejected, and when the slide moves forward a fresh round is fed from the magazine into the chamber. This system is superior to the straight blowback and the only means of producing a powerful but relatively compact handgun. While heavy blowback handguns such as the Astra 400 and 600 have been produced they are rather large handguns for the caliber. The locked-breech system is superior and practically every modern self-loader uses

This young shooter is displaying his skill with a John Inglis manufactured Browning High Power. The type is still in service in Afghanistan with our Canadian allies.

The Mauser Broomhandle pistol is among the greatest recreational handguns. With a sturdy action and well thought out operating system the Mauser is a timeless handgun.

this system. Exceptions such as the gas-delayed blowback Heckler & Koch P7 are too expensive to manufacture in today's market.

Browning first used a pair of swinging links as a means of unlocking the barrel. The links ran off of the barrel lugs in the rear, and the second set was attached near the front. Browning eventually replaced the double links with a single link in the great pistol of 1911, and at a later date designed a pistol without a link at all. The angled camming surfaces of the Browning High Power were copied by most makers of the century. There were exceptions; the highly rugged and reliable Russian Tokarev TT 33 is basically a Browning derivative that is among the last new designs to use the swinging link. The French MAS 35 is another design that relies heavily upon Browning. The Browning High Power was the world's first practical high-capacity magazine 9mm pistol. With a thirteen-round magazine and excellent design, the Browning proved to be a capable handgun. More Browning High Power pistols served as military handguns than any other handgun in history. At one point the High Power was used by more than one hundred of the world's armies. The High Power is still serving with allied troops in Iraq and Afghanistan.

While the German and American inventors are best known, there were other inventors who developed first-class service pistols. It is well known that the U.S. Cavalry was responsible for the grip and slide lock safeties of the Colt 1911. Mounted units were the spearhead of the Army and very influential. The grip safety of the Colt was designed to prevent the pistol from firing if dropped from a moving horse. The Polish Radom ViS wz.35 9mm pistol was among the last of its type designed for use as a cavalry pistol.

This is a wartime Luger in 9mm Luger caliber. A remarkable design, the Luger is sought out by collectors. This example is more or less reliable but care in choosing ammunition is essential.

The German Mauser C96, shown with a Mauser rifle of the same era, is unique and eye-catching. The .30 Mauser is a hard-hitting caliber even by modern standards.

While obviously inspired by the Colt 1911 and the Browning High Power, the Radom had a character all its own. The Radom adopted the angled camming surfaces of the High Power rather than the swinging link of the 1911, and it was also among the first Browning-derived pistols to use a full-length guide rod. The Radom was designed for horseback use. The Radom 9mm was drawn and the hammer cocked—there was no manual safety—and fired. While the 9mm may not be a big bore horse pistol, it cannot be faulted as far as penetration goes. The Radom features a grip safety that prevents the pistol from firing unless the grip safety is fully depressed. There is also a slide-mounted decocker that will safely drop the hammer if the pistol is cocked. This is an important advantage. The drill was to point the pistol at the earth and decock, then reholster. The Radom is well made of good material and even wartime guns are usually accurate and reliable. My example feeds all modern hollow-point bullets well and is famously accurate.

The Walther P38 is one of the most influential handguns of all time. The Walther features a double-action first-shot trigger, a slide-mounted decocker, and excellent fit and workmanship. The Walther uses the oscillating wedge lockup first seen on the Mauser C96. Our present service pistol, the Beretta 92, is in many ways a highly developed Walther P38. The primary advantage of the Beretta is its fifteen-round magazine capacity. The controls of the Walther are easier to manipulate than the Beretta, according to some shooters, and overall the Walther is an excellent all-around service pistol. The Walther P38 is probably still fighting

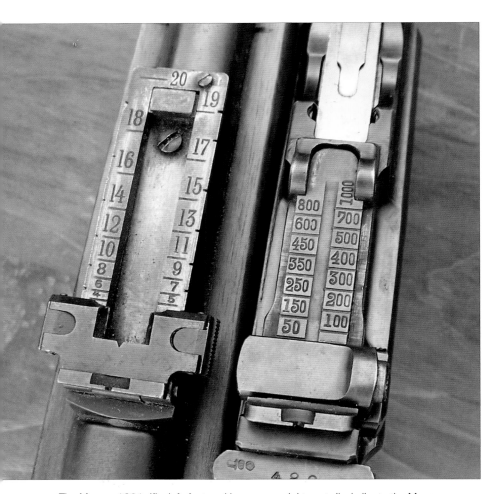

The Mauser 1891 rifle, left, featured long-range sights not dissimilar to the Mauser C96 pistol, right. Were the sights optimistic? Perhaps, but the Mauser is a fine long-range pistol.

somewhere, and I have been told that numerous armed professionals in Europe carry the P38, although it is not as popular as the Browning, Beretta, or Glock. The modern aluminum-frame variant, the P1, is a slightly modified P38 once very popular with German police forces and in substitute standard use by police forces in less advantaged nations.

By 1938 the stage was set for World War II. Germany had the Luger as standard issue. The Browning High Power had just been introduced. Produced in Belgium and Canada, the High Power was used by both sides during World War II. The French had their quirky little 7.65mm Long and the Russians had the Tokarev. The Italians had the interesting Beretta 1934 pistol in .380 ACP or 9mm Korto

Which pistol? The remarkable Heckler & Koch P7, left, is a wonderfully designed handgun while the Argentine High Power, right, is a proven war dog. Both are great handguns.

(short) caliber. America had the Colt 1911 .45. Japan had the Nambu, possibly the poorest service pistol used by any great power. Development was at a height, and during the second great bloodletting all got their blows in.

After the war, much development was afforded a new generation of service pistols. The following statement may seem simplistic, but it is true. Most nations adopted the 9mm because they had 9mm submachine guns. The Browning High Power was by far the most popular, with the Beretta 1951 enjoying reasonable sales, particularly in the Middle East. At one time the armed forces of both Israel and Egypt issued the Beretta 1951 pistol. The French adopted the MAC 50 9mm. America and Russia used proprietary cartridges, the .45 ACP and the 7.62mm Tokarev. Russia's satellite nations adopted Russian wares, although

This is the author's personal carry gun, a Springfield LW .45 with Locrian grips. While the Springfield is much improved over the original 1911, any doughboy would know how to use this modern .45.

they sometimes put their own flair into the arms. In America, there were noises concerning a new Army gun. Smith & Wesson developed the Model 39, basically an Americanized P38, but with an enclosed slide. Self-loading pistol development was rather slow until 1975, and that is where we will pick up with the modern pistols.

POCKET PISTOLS

An important part of the personal-defense scene beginning about 1900 was the manufacture of pocket pistols. These handguns were small self-loading pistols chambered for the newly developed .25 ACP or the .32 ACP. They were often well made of good material, although ironmongery was also produced. These little handguns were not powerful firearms by any means but gave the owner some peace of mind. Carried in a vest pocket, they were among the first handguns that relied more upon the threat of violence than actual killing power. No one wanted to be shot, and the possibility of death from a .25-caliber wound was all too real. Larger pistols chambered the .32 ACP and the .380 ACP. The .380 ACP was developed to give personal-defense-minded shooters a fighting chance. Some of these handguns were issued as military handguns. The French purchased millions of .32-caliber handguns during World War II, including the Savage 1910. The Savage was a well made handgun with a ten-round magazine. The advertising slogan of the Savage was "10 shots quick."

The Colt 1903 was a well made pistol that figured into many actions, particularly with the Shanghai police and was once issued to airline pilots. The safety system of the 1903 allowed cocked-and-locked carry, and the Colt 1903 was sometimes rated as superior to the Colt 1911 in design. After World War I, Walther began to develop a compact double-action first-shot pocket pistol. This pistol became known worldwide as the Walther PP or Police Pistol. The PPK is a shorter and more compact version. Originally offered in .32 ACP caliber, the PP became a popular pistol for police, for general protection, and even for the military. Versions were also offered in .380 ACP, but by far the most common is the .32 ACP. The long double-action first-shot trigger both cocked and dropped the hammer. There was no need to disengage a safety or cock the hammer before firing. The pistol's design included a combination decocking lever and safety.

The Walther is still produced today in its basic format. The Walther PP and PPK series are possibly the most successful pocket pistols ever produced. The size of pocket pistols varies widely, with the lightest pistols commonly called vest pocket pistols and the larger handguns best suited for holster carry. They are an important part of the handgunning world often overlooked by handgunners.

CHAPTER 4

Automatics: The Modern Self-Loaders

THE PROPER TERM FOR SELF-LOADING pistols is "semi-automatic." A fully automatic weapon is a machine gun, a weapon that fires multiple rounds with a single press of the trigger. We are not referring to machine guns, but since everyone calls self-loaders "automatics" we will also. We're among friends here. The term "automatic" is far less cumbersome than the more correct "semi-automatic" or "self-loading pistol." Fully automatic weapons are strictly regulated, but those wishing to go through sufficient hoops may own a fully automatic weapon. (Some feel that the anti-gunners find mistakes in nomenclature and use them against us, but just let anti-gunners read this book. I have converted more than a few or at least came to an understanding with them. After all, shooters are nice folks with an open hand to new shooters.)

The new SIG P250 is a modular design with many good features. The polymer frame offers interesting visual options. *SIGARMS*

The modern era in firearms began with the introduction of the Smith & Wesson Model 39 in 9mm caliber. A real achievement was the Model 59, which combined a high-capacity magazine with a double-action first-shot trigger. There was a lot going on in the 1970s. We will cover this shortly, but the events taking place in competition are also well worth discussion, and the evolution of handguns at this point began to be consumer driven more so than at any other time in history.

Handguns had to be appropriate to the mission and reliable to a standard never before demanded.

Behind the Soviet Bloc, the Czechs developed a number of interesting handguns. Among these was the CZ 52. This pistol fired a special hot-loaded 7.62mm Tokarev load breaking more than 1,600 feet per second. The CZ 52 used rolling cam bearings to make the pistol safe for this load. The CZ 52 is among the most accurate military handguns ever designed. Sometime later the Czechs developed the CZ 75. The CZ 75 handgun is so good Col. Jeff Cooper used the design as the basis for his combat pistol, the Bren Ten 10mm. The CZ 75 chambers the popular 9mm Luger cartridge. The trigger is double-action for the first shot. The CZ 75 in its original form is a type known as selective double-action. Although the trigger is a double-action, the pistol may be carried with the hammer cocked and safety on in the manner of the single-action 1911 handgun. An advantage is that in tactical movement, once the first shot if fired, to move safely the handgun need not be decocked but simply placed on safe.

Police departments prefer a decocker action, and later variants of the CZ 75 were supplied with a frame-mounted decocker. The CZ 75 earned a reputation as a reliable and accurate service pistol, fully the equal of anything produced

The Beretta 92 is a versatile and reliable handgun. While the design borrows heavily upon technology generally available in 1938, the quality of the Beretta combined with proven features makes it a reliable service pistol.

elsewhere in Europe. The pistol has been copied or "cloned" in the modern terminology by makers across the globe. There are variations on the safety. Some of the pistols cannot be placed on safe in the double-action mode while others may. The Armalite AR 24 is a CZ 75 clone that uniformly gives excellent service.

The SIG P229 is a credible service pistol. Compact but rugged, the P229 is praised by SIG experts such as Todd Parker.

The EAA Witness is generally reliable and accurate.

At about the same time SIG SAUER (SIGARMS) began developing its famous P Series pistols. The original P220 was a double-action first-shot 9mm with a single-column eight-round magazine. The pistol was designed to be tactically simple. There is no manual safety, only safety features. Load, decock the hammer, and fire when ready. The P220 was eventually offered in both .38 Super and .45 ACP. The P220 has been the primogenitor of many great handguns, including the P225, P226, P228, and P229. The SIG has probably been tested more than any other handgun and may well be the most reliable handgun in the world. It is certainly in the top two or three.

In Italy, Beretta was developing the Beretta 92. The Beretta 92 would go on to become a world-class pistol. The original was a selective double-action type with a frame-mounted safety. The Beretta featured a long but smooth double-action trigger and a double-column fifteen-round magazine. The pistol was produced with a slide-mounted decocker at the demand of European police who wished to be able to lower the hammer without touching the trigger. With the previous type, the hammer was steadied with the thumb or support hand and manually lowered as the trigger action was engaged.

The Beretta has gone on to great things, being adopted by the U.S. Army and many police forces. The Beretta has also given birth to many variations, including compact pistols and competition versions. In Germany. Heckler & Koch produced the first polymer-frame pistols and many other innovative designs, including the P7M8 squeeze-cocking pistol. Today, Heckler & Koch's best-selling handgun is the Universal Service Pistol, or USP. The USP has not received the military and police contracts that SIG has, largely due to the higher price of the H and K product.

The oldest design to continue to prosper is the 1911. For a pistol first delivered in 1911, the Colt and its many clones and imitators are very popular. Part of the reason for this is because of the forces exerted in competition. The 1911 was improved due to demands for better sights, a better trigger action, and better

This P220 has really been stretched. The sporting version of the P220 builds upon the inherent accuracy of the type. *SIGARMS*

handfit. The 1911 handgun has proven itself so well in the battlefields and in the streets of America, not to mention Shanghai and other hot spots, that it would seem there is little room for improvement. This may be true as a pure close-range combat handgun, but when it comes to competition and longer range fire, the 1911 needed considerable improvement.

And here is the tie in with competition: The first improved 1911s were modified by army gunsmiths for Camp Perry competition. They were fine handguns, and the army gunsmiths did a wonderful job. The factory later produced the National Match pistols and much later the acclaimed Colt Gold Cup pistols. But the real test came when Jeff Cooper and other like-minded shooters began shooting in the Big Bear California Leatherslap. These men were firing all manner of handguns, from the Colt SAA to the 1911, Luger, and double-action revolvers. The primary advantage of the fine Smith & Wesson K-38 and other revolvers over the 1911 was that the revolvers had good high-visibility sights. Considerable improvement went into the 1911. Many of these improvements were added to factory production pistols, although Colt was slow to do so. Other makers capitalized on the demand. Springfield, Kimber, and others produce first-rate 1911 handguns suited for competition and personal defense.

A pistol that took the world by storm was the Austrian Glock. Using modern manufacturing techniques, a polymer frame, and attention to detail, the Glock became popular not only with shooters but with administrators looking for the low bid. An important move made by Glock was to offer compact versions of the basic service pistol. This is a trend that has continued. Practically every service-grade handgun is offered in a compact version as well as a competition and target version with adjustable sights and often a special trigger action. At this time, it would behoove us to look at each type in turn, as they are all with us, active in the shooting sports, and definitely popular.

Let's not ignore the rimfires. Among the most important modern handguns in terms of sales and the game is the Ruger Standard Model. Introduced in 1948 at a price of $37.50, the Ruger Standard Model has become America's favorite .22-caliber handgun. Every handgunner seems to own a Ruger .22, and the pistol has done yeoman service in the training field and in competition. A number of capable target pistols are based on the Ruger Standard Model. The Browning Buckmark is also a popular handgun, well made of good material and suited for any task you would apply to a .22-caliber handgun.

There is something for everyone today. The modern pistols are so good, if I were issued my least favorite self-loading pistol I would not bemoan my fate but simply practice diligently, they are all that good, with trade-offs and advantages in each rendition. Let performance be your guide and reliability come first.

The Glock 19 9mm is among the most successful Glock pistols. The Model 19 is an abbreviated version of the Glock Model 17. *Glock Inc.*

The Heckler & Koch Universal Service Pistol is reliable and accurate. The pistol has not enjoyed the sales some types have because the HK will never be a low-bid item. *Heckler & Koch*

BERETTA

The Beretta 92 is the Army gun these days and a popular pistol in civilian use. The Beretta 92 is offered in 9mm Luger and .40 Smith & Wesson. The compact Cougar version, now offered by the Stoeger subsidiary, is offered in the same calibers. The Cougar features a rotating barrel and is a particular favorite of the author. I have enjoyed my Beretta pistols very much. They are well fitted and reliable. I have fitted a set of Hogue smooth grips to the .40 version and added a Bedair solid-steel recoil guide rod to my M9.

This is a large handgun that is difficult to conceal, but for those willing to learn the Beretta it is an accurate handgun. For International Defensive Pistol Association (IDPA) competition in the double-action class, the Beretta is competitive. Accuracy is there. I have fired a singular two-inch twenty-five-yard group with my personal M9 with Black Hills 115-grain +P ammunition. The average Beretta is an accurate, reliable handgun that is capable of protecting the owner and serving well in competition.

BROWNING

The Browning High Power is the original "wonder nine," with its thirteen-round magazine and chambered for the powerful 9mm Luger cartridge. Prior to the coming of the Browning, the 9mm was simply the German Army service cartridge. The Browning High Power put the 9mm cartridge on the map and served to make the cartridge the most popular handgun cartridge of all time.

Like many 9mm handguns, when the .40-caliber cartridge was developed, Browning produced a .40-caliber version of the High Power. The .40-caliber High Power, in my opinion, did not come off as well as some others, but the original 9mm remains the perfectly balanced and classy handgun we all know and love. Browning also produces the Buckmark .22-caliber semi auto. The Buckmark is a credible design preferred by a good number of experienced shooters. While the Buckmark .22 has merits, I keep a Buckmark on hand largely because everyone else has a Ruger! The Browning pistols are well worth your time and attention.

The P7M8 9mm is a unique squeeze cocker much sought after by professionals. You either love this one or you hate. The author loves it. *Heckler & Koch*

GLOCK

The Glock is the most popular service pistol of modern times, enjoying a position similar to that once held by the Smith & Wesson .38-caliber revolver. The Glock is not a tack driver by sporting definitions but accurate enough for self-defense. The Glock has no manual safety, only a small tab in the center of the trigger that prevents the pistol from firing under lateral pressure. This safety is primarily to prevent trigger movement and consequent firing if the Glock is dropped.

Some of us feel that the lack of a manual safety abrogates many of the advantages of the self-loading pistol. The Glock action is worth discussion. When the slide is racked, the firing pin or striker is partially cocked against spring pressure. When the trigger is pressed the striker is retracted to the point that it breaks against the sear and the pistol fires. Common wisdom tells us that the man who chooses a Glock should use the Glock and nothing else. The Glock features a fairly low bore axis, short trigger, rapid trigger reset, and steps have been taken to make the pistol fit the hands better than in early production. The Glock is a good service pistol and a good personal-defense pistol based on its own merits, but it is not the all-around do-anything go-anywhere pistol that a good 1911 handgun may be. There are competition pistols based on the Glock that given excellent results, particularly when well tuned and fitted with Warren competition sights.

The Taurus 809 is a thoroughly modern automatic pistol with many good design features. Taurus is an innovative company offering good pistols at a fair price. *Taurus*

In my experience, the Glock Model 20 10mm is the single most accurate of all Glock pistols. A drawback for the sport shooter is the polygonal rifled barrel of the Glock. This barrel features very shallow rifling. The advantages include little bullet deformation, which may aid accuracy and also higher velocity by a narrow margin than conventionally rifled barrels. The gas seal is excellent, but the polygonal design means that lead bullets are prohibited. There is nowhere for leading to build up because the grooves are quite shallow. After a time, lead buildup becomes dangerous because it will raise pressure badly. Europeans may shake their heads at Americans who use lead in their pistols, but lead bullets are an important and economical resource. The only cure for this shortcoming is to order a custom aftermarket barrel. Bar Sto and Wilson Combat are the leaders in aftermarket barrels and either will give good results. If you expect good accuracy from the Glock, the original plastic sights have to go. Warren competition sights are first class. For general use, either the Novak or Wilson Combat sights are excellent choices.

HECKLER & KOCH USP

The Universal Service Pistol began life with features that mimic the 1911 handgun, including the grip shape and frame-mounted safety. While available in double-action–only versions, the standard USP may be carried cocked and locked, hammer back, safety on. But the pistol also features a decocker. Shooters with certain hand sizes and grip styles have discovered that they inadvertently decock the handgun during a firing string. Adjustment of the grip style is mandatory when using the USP.

The USP is among the more attractive alternatives to the Glock. In common with the Glock, the steel slide and low-weight polymer frame of the USP sometimes lead to shooting low. The pistol demands practice and like the Glock must be learned. H and K produces several first-class target-grade handguns in the expert line that are a joy to own and fire and have proven very accurate.

SIG P SERIES

Lets get the obvious out of the way: The SIG is often expensive, but it is a very good handgun. When have you been sorry that you purchased quality? The SIG is generally regarded as the smoothest of all double-action first-shot pistols. The pistol is very reliable. As for accuracy, a few years ago I fired several five-shot twenty-five-yard groups with my SIG P220, using the Black Hills 230-grain JHP loading. The single-best group measured only 15/16 inch! Average groups with quality ammunition often hover around 1.5 inches. The only drawback to the SIG, and one that keeps it out of competition, is the slow trigger reset. This is noticeable only to very accomplished shooters, however.

When you fire the SIG, the trigger reset simply means you are not likely to double and fire two rounds unless you truly mean to fire two rounds. The SIG also has a high-bore centerline over the hand, but on the other hand the well designed S-curve grip keeps the recoil pushing straight back. Like all double-action pistols, the trigger

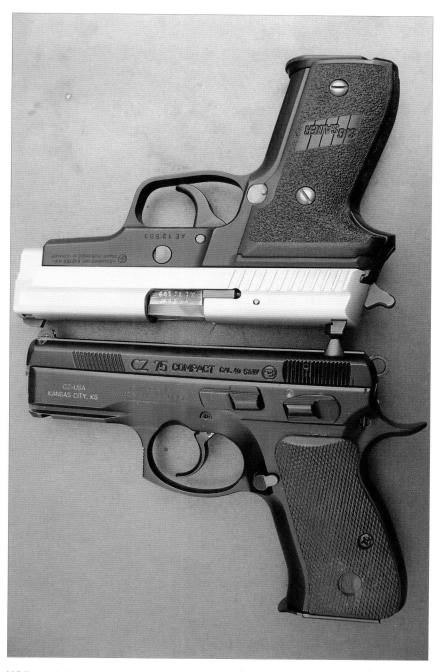

While marketing types make much of the differences between handguns, the CZ 75 and the SIG P229 are tactically identical. One will do much the same the other will. The author prefers the CZ but only by a margin.

finger rides above the trigger, on the frame, and must sweep down to engage the trigger. The P220 is a great pistol for those willing to learn the type. I have carried the P220 and the P226 on duty as a uniformed officer and have the greatest confidence in either. The dedicated SIG shooter often finds the P229 compact as the ultimate example of SIG excellence. SIG offers several sport and target versions of the P series that have given good service and proven well suited to recreational shooting.

SMITH & WESSON

Smith & Wesson's big news is the Military and Police (M&P) line, designed to compete with the Glock pistol. While these handguns have been in production only a few years, they are going to make Glock live hard! The pistols are similar to the Glock as far as the polymer frame-and-steel slide, but the pistols are unique in regard to the trigger action and slide configuration. The great advantage of the M&P is in the grip frame. The large-frame Glock .45 is simply too large for most hand sizes. An average-size hand cannot properly grasp and control such a large pistol. It is one thing to fire a handgun comfortably on the range but quite another to properly control the piece and maintain retention with cold or sweaty hands.

The .45-caliber M&P leaves nothing to be desired in this regard. I have fired my personal M&P extensively, even performing a home-grown trigger job to make the pistol a bit smoother in operation. I am enthusiastic concerning the M&P with my personal example nearing 10,000 rounds. The brass is not going to purchase a high-end pistol for police duty; the bean counters are interested in the low bid. This means a double-action–only polymer-frame pistol. If we are going that route, the M&P is the first choice. It is that good. And on a final note, the M&P is available with a well designed safety that prevents the trigger from engaging the sear when the safety is activated. This safety falls under the thumb easily. This feature alone puts the Smith & Wesson head and shoulders above any handgun without a manual safety.

TAURUS

Taurus offers clones of the 1911 and the Beretta 92 that have good features and even advantages over the originals in some regards. They have also presented

The Glock Model 17 is shown in the latest version known as the Fourth Generation. The Glock Model 17 is among the most successful handguns of all time.

the public with innovative designs of their own manufacture. I have seen quite a few of the PT99 pistols, a clone of the Beretta 92 but with adjustable sights, in service. These are excellent all around 9mms that will not break the bank. The big news from Taurus is the 24/7 polymer-frame service pistol. From its inception, the 24/7 was offered in Pro or sporting versions with a long barrel. The trigger action is smooth, and the pistol has proven as accurate as any other polymer-frame 28-ounce pistol.

I have tested the types in 9mm, .40, and .45 with the 9mm proving to be particularly accurate. In the Philippines, the Taurus PT92 9mm recently won a grueling test of service pistols to be adopted by the national police. I am waiting for the 24/7 to endure a similar test before recommending the type for police service, but at the moment the 24/7 looks good. There are other Taurus handguns that are models of efficiency and affordable. The 24/7, however, is among the most impressive new handguns introduced by any maker in the last days of the twentieth century.

RUGER

Ruger offers a dirt tough self-loader with good features. The new 345 pistol is partially well suited for general shooting chores, a considerable improvement over the previous P90 and P89 handguns. The Ruger self-loaders were designed at

The Smith & Wesson Military and Police is a bright new player in the police market. This is the author's well worn .45 caliber version.

the bloom of the 10mm fad and originally intended to handle this high-pressure cartridge. As such, standard handgun cartridges are a breeze for the Ruger to digest in harvest quantities. The Ruger appeals to the man or woman who may not wish to invest the time and ammunition needed to master a Glock or 1911 handgun but who wishes to own a high-quality handgun. The Ruger will perform with reliability and if pride of ownership means rugged appearance and the willingness to do work, the Ruger has this in spades.

Let me make a plug for the Ruger P94 pistol. This is the only .40-caliber pistol that is more accurate than the 9mm and .45-caliber versions of the basic handgun. The P94 has more style than the other 9mm pistols. Ruger also has introduced a double-action–only pistol, the SR17, which has proven particularly popular and seems off to a good start. Ruger has tremendous brand loyalty. Those who use Ruger rifles often turn to the Ruger pistols as well, and their ruggedness will often overshadow the clunky feeling some attribute to the type.

SPRINGFIELD

Springfield offers a line of 1911s that includes the single most proven 1911 of all time, the Springfield Professional. The Professional was tested by the FBI to

An interesting facet of the pistol market is that all makers must offer a tactical model to be competitive. This is a Taurus version. *Taurus*

the tune of 20,000 rounds of ammunition without a single failure. The advantages of the 1911 are many, and Springfield, once an upstart, is now an old-line company. Springfield also offers the XD pistol. This is Springfield's entry into the polymer-frame service pistol competition. It has not been adopted by police agencies, largely because the XD is actually a single-action design with safety features. The XD is a popular alternative to the Glock pistol.

KIMBER

Kimber produces first-quality 1911 handguns in a wide variety. The Custom II is as good a 1911 as offered by anyone, and while there are Kimber 1911 handguns with more features and that are tightly fitted, the Custom II is a good 1911 handgun and the original Kimber that rocked the 1911 world. The Custom Defense Pistol (CDP) is a good concealed-carry handgun with all of the features needed in a carry gun. Among the best factory custom 1911 handguns ever offered is the Kimber Gold Combat. Along with the Gold Target the Gold Combat is a high-end 1911 with everything anyone could reasonably ask. If I could own only one 1911, it would be a Kimber.

CHAPTER 5

Revolvers:
The Best of the
Modern Revolvers

SMITH & WESSON AND COLT were each founded before the Civil War. For many years they had the world revolver market wrapped up. While Europeans offered the rugged Webley and the remarkable LeFauchex, British officers often preferred American revolvers. During World War I and again in World War II, the Brits used our revolvers by the millions.

Today the scene is very different. Ruger and Taurus offer workmanlike revolvers that are a tribute to modern engineering practice. Colt is no longer a force in the revolver market save for a few custom shop items. Modern revolvers are the best ever produced for competition hunting and personal defense. I realize that some may look askance at the author for making this statement. Are modern revolvers

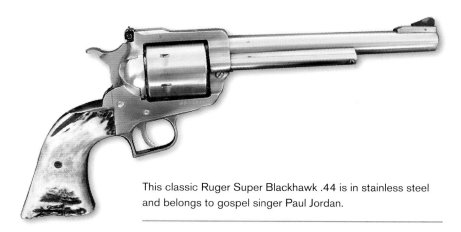

This classic Ruger Super Blackhawk .44 is in stainless steel and belongs to gospel singer Paul Jordan.

This Taurus revolver has a caliber of .454 Casull. Note the five-shot cylinder for added strength. *Taurus*

better than the Triple Lock or Five Screw? Yes, and this bold statement may easily be qualified. Modern CNC machining and tight quality control have made the modern revolver a model of precision. This is particularly true when it comes to cylinder throats and the barrel leade.

The automatic is first in combat but seldom seen in the hunting field. The perception of a revolver as a secondary handgun type is laid to rest by a trip to the hunting field or target range, or by looking in the ankle holster of a working cop. Revolvers have advantages that are primarily related to reliability, and a secondary advantage is they are usually very accurate. The modern revolver is a refined piece of machinery well worth its position in the hearts and minds of professional shooters, hunters, and adventurers. I will not mire myself in the revolver-versus-automatic debate as I use either when appropriate.

Some of the improvements in modern revolvers are obvious, others are more subtle. There are good cartridges introduced for different needs. The .32 H&R Magnum is a fine small-game cartridge for modest-sized revolvers. The .454 Casull is a giant of a cartridge, well suited to any game in North America. But we also have the even larger and more powerful .500 Smith & Wesson Magnum. Some of the cartridges and handguns are not necessarily practical for every shooter, but rather they are the showboat for the company, similar to a NASCAR racer. Only a few highly determined shooters will master the .500 Smith & Wesson. The .480 Ruger is another success story, specialized but useful. These are pure hunting handguns with little usefulness beyond the game field. That is as it should be, as the more specialization the more efficient the revolver is.

I have said that we build some things simply because we can. That may be true of some of the modern revolvers. Do we need twelve-inch barrel revolvers? The Taurus revolver may be the handgun equivalent of the Long Tom shotgun, but it is a fun piece to handle and fire. That is enough for most of us. With all of these super powerful hunting handguns available, some of us still holster the .44 Magnum. It is

The Taurus .44 Magnum with long barrel and six-shot cylinder is among the finest hunting revolvers ever built. The .44 Magnum is as heavy a cartridge as most of us will ever need.

the rare man who feels limited by the .44 Magnum and proceeds to master the .454 Casull, but he exists and commands respect.

METAL WORK

Gunmakers seldom base the efficiency of a product solely on the metal used, unlike custom knife makers who are keen to invent a particular formulation and then sweep the market. I recall the early days of ATS 34 in knife making and now it is mundane. Many makers of fine handguns will not discuss metallurgy at all except in a carefully prepared media statement. Just the same, we are assured that modern steel is better than ever. The handguns have a greater safety margin. With the Magnum cartridges so endearing to us constantly being tweaked for more velocity and more power, a safety margin is a good thing.

Those who handload are an intelligent bunch, but we have seen revolvers bent and twisted. The modern breed—both revolver and handloader—seems made of better stuff. You may still flatten a primer, but you must work hard to tie up the gun.

There are also many examples of ultra-light materials in handguns. Aluminum-frame handguns were light enough for my use, but titanium and scandium are important additions to the modern revolvers. There are issues involved in controlling such a light handgun in rapid fire and these are revolvers to be carried often and fired little. With the ever-present possibility of attack by animals, the lightweight but powerful revolver is an important addition to the explorer's or fisherman's kit. I would not wish to face a mad grizzly under any conditions, but with a lightweight .454 or .44 on my hip, I would feel that the odds were better than with tooth and nail. I am aware of a half dozen such attacks adjudicated in favor of the handgunner, but in every case it was a close thing. In the majority of cases the revolver was pressed against the body of the attacking bruin after he bowled the victim over. The revolver may be pressed against the body of the bear and the trigger pressed repeatedly. This is not possible with a self-loading pistol. Feral dogs and the big cats are another danger best addressed with a Magnum revolver.

The lower barrel is what is referred to as a pencil barrel. The upper barrel is the typical heavy Magnum-style revolver barrel.

Other improvements include modifications to the traditional ramp front sights. Sights designed for short-range use may be shorter, thicker, and stronger. The rear sights are often capable of excellent adjustment. It is unusual to see one of these modern sights out of adjustment or sprung in the track as sometimes happened with previous types. As an example, the rear sight of my personal Taurus M 44 .44 Magnum has held up through thousands of rounds of full-power Magnum ammunition. Even the cylinder latches are improved in modern revolvers. The previous design sometimes gave a bad cut to the thumb when fired with Magnum ammunition. Designed for use with rather mild cartridges, the cylinder latch was possessed of sharp edges. The modern cylinder

This young shooter is well armed with a Charter Arms .44 Special revolver. The double-action revolver remains a fine choice for all around use.

latch is somewhat modified. If you own an older revolver, the Action Works (Don Williams of Chino Valley, Arizona) will cut and polish your cylinder latch as part of a revolver package.

THE ACTION: HEART OF A REVOLVER

Modern revolvers feature a shorter hammer throw and faster lock time than any previous revolver. Despite the butter-smooth action of a 1950s Model 27, the modern revolvers are often better suited for both fast work and long-range accuracy. The hammer simply falls more quickly. During the 1930s, the legendary D. W. King and Walter King—who were not related—did custom short-action modifications to period revolvers. The primary work on the action was to shorten the hammer fall, increasing accuracy and making the double-action press shorter.

After World War II, Smith & Wesson introduced a new "short action." Naturally some of the old-timers cried about the change, but the new revolvers were more accurate and more reliable as well. Colt conversions were so well accepted that Colt introduced a factory version of the super-custom revolvers. This new pistol was the legendary Python. The makers listen and will supply the customer's wants.

Occasionally the factory produces a special edition of one Magnum or the other. This is a long-barrel Smith & Wesson 629 .44 Magnum. *Smith & Wesson*

This is a custom shop Smith & Wesson revolver. The eight-shot cylinder is obvious. This is a thoroughly modern handgun. *Smith & Wesson*

Modern revolvers often feature heavy-barrel underlugs that add weight to dampen recoil as well as protecting the ejector rod. There has been a certain revival of pencil-barrel revolvers without this underlug, but the popular heavy-barrel revolvers are the best shooters. The lighter revolvers are better suited to personal defense or for long hikes on far away trails.

Another great advantage in technology is the recoil absorbing and hand-fitting grip panels. The round butt design has become more popular than the traditional square butt. All square-butt Smith & Wesson revolvers are actually round-butt frames with square-butt grips. The better designed a grip is, the more comfortable. In some cases, we are even able to lower the bore axis, making for better control.

For the most part, the primogenitors of modern revolvers were midframe or heavy-frame revolvers originally designed for the .38 Special cartridge in the case of the midframe revolvers and the .44 Special in the case of the heavy-frame revolvers. These were mild-recoiling calibers designed primarily for accuracy. In order to handle the .357 Magnum and .44 Magnum cartridges, these frames have had the barrels, lock work, and sights constantly updated. Without these improvements we would not be able to use such loads as the 300-grain Black Hills JHP in the .44 Magnum or the Federal 180-grain JHP in the .357 Magnum without predictable parts breakage. The tightening and hardening may not be noticeable when handling the revolver, but it is evident when the revolver is put to hard use.

Some of the special editions are a little odd, but worth their weight in gold to the man or woman who needs them. This is a .357 Magnum Smith & Wesson with a built-in barrel compensator. *Smith & Wesson*

The double-action revolver mechanism is simple enough but must be timed properly. This is a Dan Wesson revolver.

As good as these big burly revolvers are, a number of startling improvements have come about in the small-frame concealed-carry revolvers. Small and light is more than a watchword, it is the bottom line. Small and light is good for carry, but if you actually practice with the handgun recoil becomes a consideration. A great deal of work had gone into designing a proper grip frame and the stocks for the grip frame to allow the shooter to use powerful lightweight handguns well. Among the great success stories for Smith & Wesson is the concealed-carry Centennial type revolver as exemplified by the Model 442. With a concealed hammer, the revolver is snag-free on the draw. This is important in pocket carry. Taurus and Charter Arms have also produced revolvers with a concealed hammer. The geometrically designed inner hammer is reliable, and the humpback grip frame of these revolvers is more comfortable than a conventional grip frame. They are double-action–only designs with no visible hammer to cock. An important advantage is that the concealed hammer revolver may be fired from the pocket with no danger of a malfunction.

FIGHTING WITH RECOIL

Modern revolvers often feature smoother edges that make for more comfortable shooting when recoil is heavy. The light revolvers with concealed hammers feature a grip frame that moves the hand higher on the grip and makes the grip more comfortable.

No matter what the grip shape, the scandium and titanium-frame handguns will take a bite when they are fired. These revolvers demand attention to detail and practice. They are light and handy and have more energy for ounce than any other handgun type.

OPINIONS

To qualify my opinions on modern revolvers, I fired quite a few. I have to admit I was impressed with every revolver I fired. The small personal-defense revolvers are well made of good material, but the large-frame revolvers arrested my interest. The modern revolvers are more precise than anything I have used in the past. With CNC machining and strict quality control, these revolvers are capable of excellent accuracy with quality ammunition.

I cannot honestly say that the modern .454 revolvers are as comfortable to shoot as a .44 Magnum, but with the modern heavy underlug barrel the weight has a dampening effect on recoil. Couple this with rubberized grips, and you have a firearm capable of great accuracy and one that is comfortable to fire. I have fired a singular two-inch fifty-yard group with the Taurus Raging Bull in .454 Casull and Cor Bon ammunition. With attention to detail and confidence, it can be done. Despite fierce recoil, eddies did not appear in my flesh. I tolerated the recoil and concentrated on the sight picture—the combined view of gun sights and target and the correct placement of sights on the target. The rest is history.

The revolver illustrated is a Charter Arms .44 Special Bulldog. It is fitted with a modern add-on light rail.
Laser Lyte

FASTER RELOADING

One of the criticisms of the revolver is that it is slow to reload and has limited capacity. This means little in the hunting field, but today we have modern revolvers with seven- and eight-round cylinders. The little .22s have often been available with nine-shot cylinders, but the big bores are catching up. As a bonus, the lock time of some of these revolvers is faster due to modifications to the lock work to accommodate a seven-shot cylinder as with the modern .357 Magnum L-frame Smith & Wesson. Speed loaders are also available, and they are a great asset for the revolver shooter. They demand practice, but with the proper technique speed loaders are very fast.

Speedloaders were first patented in 1877 to the best of my knowledge. Before that date, tactically minded souls carried a spare cylinder for their cap-and-ball revolver. British troops deployed revolver speed loaders as early as 1902. With the Webley .455 revolver and its very fast break-top action, these soldiers were the best armed in the world at that date as far as fast reloading went. The fastest reload of all belongs to the Smith & Wesson .45 Auto Rim revolver with moon clips. The moon-clipped revolver is often used in competition and remains the fastest revolver to reload, period.

During World War I there was a shortage of 1911 autoloaders. Smith & Wesson and Colt revolvers were in full production for the British in .455 caliber. It was a simple matter to reengineer the revolver to chamber the .45 ACP cartridge. There is no case rim for the ejector star to grab and eject. Smith & Wesson invented a special shim that held three cartridges. These were called half-moon clips. They allowed the .45 ACP cartridge to properly headspace in the revolver. Best of all, they could be loaded quickly. When the revolver was fired, all that was needed was a quick flick of the ejector rod to unload it. With conventional cartridges, even a speedloader is much slower. If the revolver is not held perfectly muzzled up, there is a chance of the cartridge case hanging under the ejector star; moon clips eliminate this problem. Even with the muzzle down the moon clips ejected.

Today, we have two-, three-, and six-shot clips. The full-moon clip is especially popular, and suppliers such as Beckham Design offer polymer clips. Ranch Products has served the author for years with steel full-moon clips. The Taurus Tracker is a modern compact revolver with a five-shot capacity that is also available in .45 ACP with a special moon clip. There

Ruger Magnum revolvers are famed for accuracy. This young shooter is sizing up the Ruger with its optical sight. Note Uncle Mike's shoulder holster.

The Taurus four-inch barrel .357 Magnum revolver belongs to a versatile class of revolvers. This revolver may use both .38 Special and .357 Magnum ammunition. *Taurus*

are eight-shot .38 Super and .357 Magnum revolvers that use special fast-loading clips. The .45 ACP, .38 Special, and .357 Magnum are versatile cartridges. These cartridges will accomplish anything that really needs to be done in competition or personal defense, and the revolvers chambering these cartridges are first class, accurate handguns.

Modern revolvers are models of modern manufacture. The advantages of the revolver, including reliability and handling, are more apparent that ever in the modern versions of the wheelgun. It is interesting to note that older self-loaders may be modified to a more modern standard given sufficient dedication and funds. But an older revolver simply cannot be brought up to modern standards. You will need to purchase a new revolver to reap the benefits of the modern technology behind them.

CHAPTER 6

General-Purpose Handguns

I HOPE THE PREVIOUS CHAPTERS HAVE whetted your interest in handguns. While history is interesting, we are now moving on to practical application. I am an all-around handgunner with broad interests: I enjoy studying the mechanical aspects of handguns and their history and gauging the practical applications of each type. I enjoy hand loading ammunition for its own sake, and I enjoy hunting. I love an accurate, friendly .22-caliber pistol. But when it comes to choosing a handgun to win a match, protect my hide, or take game, I have the most stringent criteria.

There is no denying the laws of physics: big bores do more work. Big bullets let out more blood and let more air into the wound. When learning to master the handgun, be aware that you are working your way toward a suitable big bore, whether you are a hunter or a personal-defense shooter. Even in target shooting, there are great advantages in the well-mannered big bores such as the .44 Special revolver cartridge and the .45 ACP automatic

Often a pistol is a highly personal item. This Colt Gold Cup features custom grips from JMB Distribution. They were done by a respected artist. Note Ward Leather Company gear. This is a very special kit.

Double-action revolvers still command respect. The 2.5-inch barrel Combat Magnum, top, sports Pachmayr grips for concealed carry, while the lower revolver, a 4-inch barrel Combat Magnum, sports recoil absorbing Hogue MonoGrips.

cartridge. The calibers that begin with the number four are by far the most efficient all-around performers for heavy use. As soon as you are able mentally, physically and financially, you should graduate to a big bore handgun.

I have often stated that the three most useful calibers are the .22 for practice, the .44 Magnum for game, and the .45 ACP (.45 Automatic) for bad guys. Nothing has changed my mind. But it would be foolish not to recognize that the .38 Special and 9mm Luger have a place in the scheme of things. They are all of the cartridge many shooters are willing to master.

In some situations the caliber is more important than the handgun. In you are a rancher in Montana, a farmer in Mississippi, or a hiker in Vermont, your handgun choice may be different but the problem you face is similar. You need a good general-purpose handgun well suited to many pursuits. I have narrowed the field to a relative handful of handguns that will make a find general-purpose handgun for all-around use. There is a common thread in each handgun, and that is versatility. None are too large or too small. That is a key to choosing a handgun. It should not remind you of a boat anchor and be uncomfortable during your daily movement, but it should not be so small that it is inefficient. Here's an example: While a hunting handgun with an 8 3/8-inch barrel is efficient, you will not carry it hiking for defense against bears. A target-grade Glock with the long barrel will not fit into the scheme of things in urban defense.

The first requirement of a general-purpose handgun is quality. The sidearm must be well made of good material with a good reputation for reliability. The handgun must be ergonomic. The grip frame must be comfortable, the controls

The SIG P220 is easily among the most reliable handguns ever made. SIG fans may justly claim their choice is among the finest made handguns in the world.

This modern cylinder latch is leagues ahead of the older styles. This latch is designed to be less abrasive when firing heavy loads.

well placed for rapid manipulation, and the handgun must offer a smooth, consistent trigger action. The handgun must be accurate enough for the intended chore. Accuracy has several facets, including practical accuracy, which is how well we are able to use the piece off hand, and intrinsic accuracy, which is basic mechanical accuracy. A group is the standard measure of accuracy but a group never saved a life. On-demand accuracy is what counts.

The Glock Model 21 .45-caliber pistol is a fine choice for Glock fans. Accurate, reliable, and holding fourteen rounds of hard-hitting ammunition, the Glock is a fine all-around handgun. *Glock Inc.*

A general-purpose handgun or an all-around handgun should place five shots into three inches or less on demand at twenty-five yards. An accurate handgun will challenge the interested shooter. The handgun must be powerful enough to accomplish the task at hand whether the task is taking small game with head shots or taking deer-size game at fifty yards. With this criteria, I regard the .357 Magnum as a starting point in an all-around handgun. The .357 Magnum, with good loads such as the Black Hills 158-grain JHP, kills out of proportion to its size. The .357 is versatile. You may load a light target-grade wadcutter at 750 feet per second for practice and small game or deploy a 180-grain bullet at more than 1,200 feet per second for large game. This is the small-bore cartridge I simply cannot fault.

With a balance that favors urban use, the all-around handgun should not weigh more than thirty-five ounces for constant carry. With the occasional foray into hiking, a lightweight .357 Magnum revolver seems ideal. There are more powerful revolvers, but they are also more difficult to control well. For treks into snake country I often load the first chamber of my revolver with a CCI Speer snake shot round. Thus loaded, I am ready for anything that slivers. With this criteria in mind, the first all-around handgun is the four-inch barrel .357 Magnum revolver. Relatively lightweight, with good accuracy and great versatility, the four-inch barrel .357 on the medium-frame is a good choice for most of us.

THE FOUR-INCH BARREL .45 COLT REVOLVER

A superior package is found with the four-inch barrel Smith & Wesson revolver in .45 Colt. The four-inch barrel is accurate enough for practically any chore yet relatively fast to clear leather. The .45 Colt cartridge, when carefully hand loaded, is capable of taking deer-sized game to fifty yards and black bear and boar at close range. The .45 Colt isn't as versatile as the .44 Magnum for some uses but packs plenty of horsepower. This is a grand revolver and a favorite of many shooters. It is wise to stay within the 23,000-psi range when hand loading for this cartridge. If you need a Magnum get one! While a fine all-around revolver, this one is best reserved for hand-loaders.

4x44

The 4x44 is a four-inch barrel .44 Magnum. While a bear to control, the possibilities are almost limitless. This combination will take medium-sized game but may be concealed under a long coat given the proper leather. For those who favor the revolver, the .44 Magnum is a versatile choice even if limited to factory ammunition. The Taurus M 44 is a particular favorite in my family. The recoil-absorbing rubber grips are a great aid in controlling the handgun.

This is my wife's favorite defense and sporting revolver. She loads it with the Speer .44 Special Gold Dot JHP as a bedside gun and one my .44 Magnum hand-loads when we travel in choice country. (I use the Nosler 240-grain JHP.) The sights are a model of rugged perfection. The M 44 features conservative barrel ports that are a great aid in controlling recoil, while offering a modest cut in velocity. The 4x44 is among the most versatile of portable handguns for hunting, personal defense, and sports such as bowling pin shooting and silhouette matches.

The author's family relies upon a handful of capable revolvers. Jessie is firing the Taurus M 44 revolver in .44 Magnum.

THE SIX-INCH BARREL .44 MAGNUM

I have used both the heavy underlug 629 Classic .44 Magnum and the lighter barrel Model 629 .44 Magnum extensively. The six-inch barrel adds sixty to one hundred feet per second in velocity to Magnum loads, and the long sight radius is an aid in long-range accuracy. The 629's lighter weight makes for easier packing, while the Classic is noticeably easier to shoot well. These .44 Magnums are heavy but when the feet leave the pavement they are comforting.

This is a stainless-steel Smith & Wesson Model 625 revolver. This example has been specially modified by Fletcher Custom, a shop with a good reputation. *Fletcher Custom*

The odds do not favor a four-legged attack, but you and I do not wish to be the person who drowned in a stream with an average depth of three feet. Bear attacks occur with regularity, and the big cats seem increasingly aggressive. Despite the advice of those who should know better, playing dead will simply get you killed. Well-known bear expert Timothy Treadwell did just that, and he is no longer with us. The unfortunate attack and killing of a young woman by a pack of coyotes is also disturbing. If you are an outdoors person then consider every use the handgun may be put to and choose from this list. If hunting is a real need, the six-inch barrel .44 Magnum is a great choice. For personal defense in a full-power .44 Magnum load the 165-grain Cor Bon JHP is ideal. At the opposite end of the Spectrum the 320-grain Cor Bon loads are superb penetrating loads.

THE ULTRA LITE

I have been able to test a number of the Ultra Lite or Scandium-frame .44 Magnum revolvers. I will not sugarcoat the facts; these handguns are brutal to fire. In recoil they rise over the brow. Nonetheless, I have fired them enough to state that they are reliable and could be a superbly efficient lifesaver in bear country, loaded with a credible choice such as the Black Hills 300-grain JHP. However, few writers have noted that this lightweight revolver is among the most packable and easy to carry of all big-bore revolvers and a good choice for personal defense when loaded with the .44 Special Speer Gold Dot. This makes for an interesting option and a coun-terpoint to everyone else's automatic.

If your tastes run more to urban carry and personal defense you obviously do not need a heavy Magnum revolver. But you may wish to own something that is versatile enough to defend the home, your person, your curtilage against animals, and also to engage in meaningful target practice and even competition. This may seem a tall order, something like driving the family sedan to Daytona and winning

With its heavy-barrel underlug, the Smith & Wesson Model 629 is a well balanced hunting revolver. Relatively light but powerful, the 629 is a great hunting revolver.

the 500, then going camping in Baja. The fact is, there are any number of competitions that invite service-grade handguns to compete. But you will not be competitive with a too small pocket pistol, and you may not be competitive in a fight for your life either. Lets look at some of the best choices.

SIG P220 .45

The SIG is a relatively compact double-action first-shot pistol. The SIG is possibly the most accurate production pistol available in its class. The SIG P220 is the most accurate of the

This AirLite Smith & Wesson .44 isn't a handgun for beginners. For those who truly need a light and powerful .44 Magnum revolver, the AirLite is a reasonable choice.

SIG pistols I have fired. If you cannot tolerate cocked-and-locked carry, and many cannot for good reasons, the SIG will be a better choice for you than the 1911. The pistol is smooth and reliable and is proven in difficult military trails. The ergonomics are good and the pistol is a favorite of seasoned handgunners.

GLOCK MODEL 20 10MM

The Glock Model 20 is the single most accurate large-frame Glock. I do not think anyone could give a counterpoint to his statement. I have fired groups as small as 1 1/8 inch at twenty-five yards, far better than any group I have fired with the .45-caliber Model 21. The frame is a stretch for most hands, but this doesn't matter as much in the field when you are taking deliberate shots at game. The 10mm will do things at fifty yards that cannot be done with the .45 automatic.

Load the 10mm with Cor Bon hunting ammunition, be certain to place your shot carefully, and you will have a capable handgun for deer-sized game. As for personal defense, the 135-grain Cor Bon JHP at well over 1,400 feet per second is a credible defense load. A good all-around load is the Cor Bon 155-grain DPX at 1,200 feet per second. I find that the full-power 10mm loads kick little more than the .45, but not badly, and offer good efficiency in the field. If a 15-shot Glock that offers approximately .357 Magnum levels of energy appeals to you, the Glock Model 20 is a superior handgun. The 10mm Glock is also a favorite competition handgun in use by top shooters such as Eddie Wagoner.

THE GLOCK 21

The big-frame Glock has one main fault. It is too large for most hands. This doesn't mean as much in a sporting gun, but in a handgun to be used for personal defense it means everything. For those who are able to handle the girth of the grip, the Glock Model 21 .45 is among the lightest kicking .45-caliber service pistols available. The pistol has a good reserve of ammunition and has proven reliable. While not as accurate as the 10mm Glock Model 20, most modern Model 21s will group five shots into two to three inches at twenty-five yards with a quality load such as the Black Hills 230-grain JHP.

THE KIMBER ECLIPSE

When it comes to a single handgun that represents the modern breed of highly advanced 1911 handguns, the Kimber Eclipse is at the top of the heap. The pistol is reliable, accurate, good looking, and we could go on. The Eclipse also features adjustable sights. Adjustable sights are essential for the sport shooter. The sights may be zeroed for 185-grain hunting loads, 200-grain target loads, and 230-grain personal-defense loads. The Eclipse is a good piece that will get you through the night, even if the night is filled with nightmares. Plus there is a certain pride of ownership in owning such a well made pistol.

SPRINGFIELD LIGHTWEIGHT LOADED MODEL

This is simply the Loaded Model .45 with an aluminum frame. Recoil is increased, but the long sight radius of the Government Model 1911 is retained. The pistol handles well, is fast into action, and most of all carries light on the hip. While it isn't in the cards that you will control this pistol as well on a combat course, for the few shots that matter the LW .45 hits as hard as any.

BERETTA 92 9MM

I am not enthusiastic concerning the 9mm Luger cartridge, but some people are. The Beretta 92 is a proven reliable handgun. The Beretta 92 is often used in the appropriate matches at IDPA. The Beretta is widely available, accessories are plentiful, leather gear is available off the shelf, and the pistol is accurate enough for any foreseeable use. If you have confidence in the 9mm round—read Winchester SXT +P or +P+—you have an ideal platform for all-around use. There is something satisfying about deploying the same pistol used by our soldiers in any number of actions and full-blown wars since 1981. The Beretta, properly maintained, is as reliable as any machine may be.

FINAL WORDS

Say what you will about the great handguns, no one has matched American inventors as far as ergonomics, flair, and design. The French created quirky monstrosities, and the Spanish excelled in ironmongery. The Germans occasionally got it right, while the Japanese had no clue.

Samuel Colt and John Moses Browning understood human engineering. Ergonomics is often used interchangeably with human engineering, but they are

This SIG P220 .45 is plain but effective. Carried in a DeSantis IWB holster, the powerful P220 is first-class protection.

This young soldier is making the Beretta 92 talk. This is perhaps the most controllable of the service 9mms, even with the powerful Black Hills +P loading.

This is another example of a custom .45 and quality leather. The grips are from Locrian Customs and the leather is from CCO, Collins Custom Leather. This is first-class gear well worth the price.

not quite the same thing. Ergonomics describes an object's compatibility with a human user. It takes a shooter to design a shooting iron. When handguns made the shift from single shot to repeater, ergonomics became much more important. The hand had to grasp the pistol, the thumb cocked the hammer, and the trigger finger pressed the trigger. While the single-action design is dated, you can't fault the handling. It is easy to grasp the handle and hold it comfortably. The handgun has a natural point. This is ergonomics. The slow loading speed is a design feature, not a human engineering defect.

The break-top Smith & Wesson revolver wasn't in the same league. The European single-actions such as the Mauser left one wondering why? Double-action revolvers introduced a whole new host of problems. The trigger reach could not stretch the average hand, while the hand had to be stabilized; the palm could not slip as the trigger finger operated the action. Double-action revolvers were not very handy until Smith & Wesson introduced the Hand Ejector in 1899. The Hand Ejector later became the Military and Police revolver. This revolver is the ideal size, fast into action and with a natural balance. Smith & Wesson got it right.

This is the handgun that the late Tom Ferguson, a police writer of some reputation, called the "Gunfighter's Gun of the Twentieth Century." Worn on the hip in a Threepersons or Ranger holster with just the right "Cowboy Slant," the M&P revolver is handy and fast into action. There may be more powerful revolvers but none that handle in a superior manner.

About 1900, John Moses Browning began developing a line of automatic pistols for Colt Firearms and also for Fabrique Nationale. The Colt 1900 pistol fully enclosed the barrel with a new invention, the pistol slide. This slide was a block against foreign material. Contrast this design with the Luger and you will see how revolutionary the Colt pistol was. The next great ergonomic handgun was the Colt Model of 1911, usually referred to simply as the 1911.

The 1911 is the most superbly handling pistol ever produced. The ergonomics are excellent, and while the pistol is not the best for every purpose, it is the best fighting pistol. From the most accurate and not in the running for most powerful, the 1911 is a fast-handling handgun designed to kill enemy soldiers quickly.

The 1911 was designed for fast handling off of horseback. The controls fall under the digits easily. The slide lock safety, slide latch, and magazine catch are all within easy reach of an average-sized hand. Manipulation is positive. The grip safety funnels the hand into the grip frame, and with a proper firing grip you will depress the safety. But if the handgun is dropped with the safety off, the pistol will not fire due to the blocking action of the grip safety. In terms of human engineering, the pistol cannot be faulted. When the Colt was developed actions in the Philippines had shown a need for a handgun capable of stopping multiple adversaries quickly. The cavalry was an influential part of the armed services that needed the best pistol possible. These men depended upon a good pistol to keep them alive in a hostile environment.

The 1911 offers rapid replenishment of the ammunition supply by a movement as simple as placing the hands together. The pistol may be reloaded while pointed at an adversary. There are few sharp edges.

For most applications the 1911 or the M&P in their many variations are good choices. The revolver now has adjustable sights and is chambered for the powerful .357 Magnum cartridge. Highly developed 1911 handguns offer gilt-edged accuracy. Both are available in compact versions. Larger handguns are less handy to handle and carry, and they are best suited for slow deliberate firing. The ergonomics of the big-frame revolvers are not as good, but if hunting is the game then they are more acceptable.

PART II

Before You Begin

CHAPTER 7

Methods of Operation

IN THIS CHAPTER WE WILL discuss how handguns work, how they are loaded and unloaded, and how they are handled. Pay close attention as there is only one safe way to handle a firearm. A working knowledge of the various types is an essential part of your handgun encyclopedia. Although there are differences in the exact procedure when each is handled, the basics of the revolver and the self-loader are the same. As an example, all automatic pistols have some type of magazine. All revolvers have a rotating cylinder. The devil is in the details. We will look at the older type, revolvers, first.

SINGLE-ACTION REVOLVERS

In the single-action revolver, the hammer must be manually cocked for each shot. When the hammer is brought to the rear against spring pressure, a notch in the hammer catches and the hammer is held in place. The trigger is pressed, tripping the sear, releasing the hammer notch. The hammer flies forward and supplies the power to crack the cap or primer and fires the revolver.

This automatic pistol is functioning properly. One spent case is in the air while another has just fired, and the slide is retracting the case from the chamber.

With a spent case is in the air, the CZ 75 is locked and ready to fire again with a press of the trigger.

When using rimfire cartridges the hammer nose struck the rim of the cartridge, smashing it against the cylinder and firing the handgun. A separate firing pin became part of the design of some revolvers, while others maintained a sharp edge of the hammer as the firing pin. Most modern revolvers now feature a transfer bar for ignition. The hammer is never in contact with the firing pin. The hammer falls forward and strikes the transfer bar, which in turn strikes the firing pin, firing the handgun.

To load the revolver, we must insert a cartridge into each cylinder. With the single-action type, this is done by opening the loading gate and inserting one cartridge at a time. With the original Colt revolvers the hammer is placed on half cock to allow the cylinder to rotate as each chamber is loaded. Modern Ruger single-action revolvers are loaded by opening the loading gate; it is not necessary to place the revolver on half-cock. This system of loading was carried on to some double-action revolvers such as the double-action Frontier Model Colt. Even as late as the 1930 there were inexpensive foreign revolvers that used gate loading in combination with a double-action trigger.

A variation on the single-action was the top-break revolver. In this design, the frame is hinged. There is a latch on the hinge that is pressed open in the Smith & Wesson manner, or in the case of the Webley, there is a long lever that operates the latch.

When the frame is unhinged, the barrel is pressed downward and automatic ejection occurs. The spent cases are sent flying free of the cylinder. It is a simple matter to insert cartridges into each cylinder at this juncture. The break-top revolver survived until relatively recent times, with the Harrington and Richardson five-shot .38-caliber Smith & Wesson revolver remaining popular at a time when most would agree it was obsolete.

The next variation is the double-action revolver with swing-out cylinder. With the double-action revolver the trigger is pressed and trigger action both cocks and drops the hammer. The trigger exerts pressure against the hammer, which works against the mainspring, and finally the hammer breaks and falls. Most double-action revolvers also have a single-action notch in the hammer. In other words, they may be cocked for a deliberate single-action shot. However, even a few very early double-action revolvers were double-action only. This simply means that the revolver could only be fired by trigger cocking. There was no single-action hammer notch. Double-action–only revolvers are popular today, particularly in the concealed-hammer versions. While a hunter may wish to take a deliberate single-action shot with his double-action revolver, most agree that speed demands that the personal-defense revolver be fired double-action at all times.

As I mentioned, the early double-action revolvers were either gate loading in the same manner as single-action revolvers or they were break-top actions. But beginning in 1889 Colt began manufacturing solid-frame swing-out cylinder revolvers. While it took some time for the break-top revolver to be phased out, the strength of the solid-frame revolver with a swing-out cylinder was an obvious advantage. With the swing-out cylinder revolver, a latch of some type is activated to allow the cylinder to be swung out away from the frame.

In early designs, including the Colt 1892 and the Smith & Wesson Hand Ejector, the ejector rod latched only at the rear of the cylinder. In later designs the cylinder is secured both front and rear. (A number of inexpensive designs still use a single-point lockup more or less successfully.) The famous Smith & Wesson Triple Lock revolvers featured a three-point lockup. Today, a number of modern Magnum revolvers lock up at three points, the third using a spring-loaded stud on the crane.

The crane is the part that the cylinder rides on. The ejector rod rides through the cylinder's central axis. When the cylinder is swung open, the cartridges are loaded in the chambers. The muzzle should be pointed down or the cartridges will slide out during this operation. After the chambers are loaded, the cylinder is pressed closed and the chamber locks in place. After the revolver is fired, the cartridge will be ejected by once again opening the cylinder and then by pressing the ejector rod to the rear to unload the spent cartridges. With practice you may unload the revolver one round at a time and replenish the ammunition supply if you have fired only a round or two.

Revolvers do not normally incorporate a manual safety, although there have been many revolvers manufactured in the past, primarily in Europe, that feature some type of safety lever. Revolvers use rebounding hammers, transfer bar actions, and other devices to ensure safety. Many early revolvers featured

The safe action Glock is available in several variations. This is the Model 37 in .45 GAP, among the best of the Glock handguns for personal defense. *Glock Inc.*

hammer-mounted firing pins that rested upon the primer of the cartridge under the hammer if the revolver was fully loaded. If you have any doubt, always keep the chamber directly under the firing pin or hammer empty. Even in modern times, five beans under the wheel is not a bad idea. Revolvers rely upon safety features more so than a manual safety. Modern revolvers are divided into two types, the single-action revolvers, which are primarily used for hunting and for sport, and double-action revolvers, which are used in hunting, competition, and personal defense. The primary advantages of the revolver are simplicity and ruggedness.

SELF-LOADERS

In historical terms, automatic is the proper term for this type of handgun. Automatic simply means the firearm is capable of firing, cycling the empty casing, stripping a fresh round from the magazine, and loading a round into the breech or

This is the Beretta M9 9mm double-action first-shot pistol. The Beretta is shown with the safety and decocker in the vsafe position.

This Beretta 92 is ready for a single-action shot, with the hammer cocked and the safety off.

chamber with a single pull of the trigger. The term "self-loading" is equally correct. Some of the descriptions of the automatic refer to the trigger-action type. These include single-action and double-action. However, the operation also is worthy of your interest.

The simplest form of operation is blowback action. In a blowback action the pistol fires and the slide recoils against spring pressure. The slide recoils until spring pressure is overcome. Along the way, the spent cartridge has been extracted and ejected by an extractor mounted on the slide. As the slide returns forward, a fresh round is stripped from the magazine by the cocking block, a lower section of the slide. The round is chambered by forward motion of the slide. All this is made

This Colt Targetsman .22 is locked open. Note that the slide—it could be called a bolt—recoils while the barrel remains fixed to the frame.

The Beretta 92 is locked open with a magazine nearby for loading. Since the Beretta is a locked-breech design the barrel has moved to the rear partially as the slide was locked open.

The Beretta 92 9mm is locked open and a magazine is about to be inserted into the grip frame. Next. the slide will be lowered to load a round into the chamber.

possible by recoil energy stored in the recoil spring, which is usually mounted under the barrel. The blowback action is then ready to fire again.

In this type of action the barrel is stationary. Blowback operation is suitable for calibers of .22 to .380 ACP. There have been a relative handful of locked-breech .380 ACP handguns. The problem with blowback operation is blowback operation does not sufficiently contain the high energy and pressure of a powerful cartridge. For this reason a handgun firing the 9mm Luger cartridge or something even more powerful must be overly large and heavy. The Astra 600 is at the upper limit of size and weight acceptable for a service pistol, and it is a blowback design. Today the inexpensive Highpoint pistol is a straight blowback, but few other full-power handguns use the blowback action.

The locked-breech action is an efficient means of controlling pressure. In this type of automatic pistol the slide and barrel recoil together as the pistol fires. This is accomplished in various ways. The Mauser pistol used an oscillating wedge. Today, the Beretta M 9 uses a similar action. The Luger uses a knee joint–like device called a toggle. The Colt 1911 uses a single swinging link that allows the barrel to tilt. The Browning High Power and practically every new design since uses the angled camming surface. The oscillating wedge and swinging link are easily the oldest systems while angled camming surfaces are more modern and more easily manufactured.

With the locked-breech system the barrel and slide recoil as a unit. Once the bullet exits, the barrel pressure is greatly alleviated. At this point the barrel's rearward motion is stopped—the link in the 1911 has met the end of its travel—and the slide continues to the rear, extracting the spent cartridge from the chamber. A frame-mounted ejector strikes the brass case, and the case is ejected from the pistol. The slide then returns forward, stripping a cartridge from the magazine and feeding it into the chamber. There are variations on the theme. Gas-operated long guns are common; pistols using gas operation are rare.

These are three of the author's home-defense handguns. Each represents a different state of readiness. The Smith & Wesson revolver at left is fired by a single long press of the trigger. The SIG, center, is fired for the first shot by a long press of the trigger. The hammer of the Kimber .45, right, must be cocked before the pistol may be fired.

The Heckler & Koch P7M8 is a blowback design but it is compact. A special gas chamber retards rear slide movement; hence the P7M8 is a gas-retarded blowback. The system obviously works for this ultra-reliable handgun.

In basic operation, the locked breech and the blowback appear similar to the untrained eye, but they differ considerably. The next important part of the pistol is the action. No matter whether the handgun is a flintlock or a modern polymer-frame handgun, there must be some way of igniting the powder charge. The first automatics were all single-action designs. This simply means that the trigger press did one thing: It dropped the hammer.

The Mauser C 96 is a single-action. The pistol is cocked and a press of the trigger fires the handgun by dropping the hammer. The Broomhandle pistol features a manual safety that is rather rifle like in operation. The first Browning type pistols did not feature a safety at all. They were single-action designs and were ready to fire once cocked. To make the pistol safe to carry, the hammer was lowered. The hammer had to be manually thumb-cocked to fire the pistol. Since we had just transitioned from single-action revolvers, this was not seen as a particular drawback. Once the hammer was cocked, each press of the trigger fired the handgun. In order to make hammer down carry safe, the inertia firing pin was developed. As late as the 1960s, and perhaps later, some pistols used firing pins that were so long that the firing pin rested upon the cartridge primer when the hammer was lowered. This is unsafe.

The inertia firing pin is shorter than the firing pin channel. As a result, when the hammer is lowered the inertia firing pin is not pressed against the primer of the cartridge. The inertia firing pin is held to the rear by firing pin spring pressure. When the hammer strikes, the firing pin is driven forward against firing pin pressure. After firing, the firing pin spring brings the firing pin back into position. Later modifications include the Polish Radom's decocker lever that safely lowers the hammer without the shooter touching the trigger. The single-action design is the first to be modified with the addition of a safety. The German Luger, a single-action design, used a sear blocking safety lever. The Colt 1911 featured a slide-lock safety that locks the slide in place and bears against the disconnect, preventing the pistol from firing.

A wise addition to these handguns was the grip safety. Unless the grip safety is completely pressed, the pistol will not fire. While used on some revolvers, the grip safety is most prevalent on handguns such as the German Luger and Colt 1911, although most Lugers were manufactured without the grip safety. The modern Springfield XD uses the grip safety.

There have been many types of actions offered as an alternative to the single-action. The primary reason is the perceived problem of a reared hammer. While I have carried the 1911 cocked-and-locked hammer to the rear and safety on for many years the fact is many are uncomfortable with this type of carry. The double-action first-shot pistol is offered as an alternative. Usually simply called the double-action pistol, the DA type uses a drawbar to transfer energy from the trigger to the hammer. The trigger is pressed and the drawbar moves the hammer to the rear. When the hammer breaks against spring pressure, the hammer falls

In this illustration a Kimber 1911 is carried in the proper condition, with the hammer back and the safety activated. The holster is a Null shell horsehide holster.

and the pistol fires. The slide cycles and the slide cocks the hammer in recoil. Subsequent shots are fired single-action. There is usually a decocking lever ala the P38 to lower the hammer without touching the trigger; however, there are alternate designs called selective double-action that operate differently.

These handguns (the CZ 75 in original format is one example) feature a positive frame-mounted safety. The pistol may be carried cocked and locked or hammer down for a double-action first shot. To lower the hammer, it is controlled with the thumb or weak side hand while the trigger is pressed and the hammer manually lowered. Administrators and general officers do not like manual lowering of the hammer, and the double-action first-shot pistol with a decocker is popular as a result. Some double-action first-shot handguns do not feature a safety, only a decocker. The SIG P220 is among the best of these. The SIG has safety features but no manual safety. The primary complaint with the double-action first-shot pistol is the length of the trigger press. Despite the manufacturers' best efforts, a double-action automatic pistol's trigger action will never be as smooth as a revolver. The revolver has greater leverage and a shorter throw. We are only moving a cylinder after all. Then there is the need to learn two trigger actions with the double-action first-shot pistol and learning the transition from double-action to single-action shooting.

The result was the introduction of various safe-action, fast-action, and double-action–only handguns. With the double-action–only every firing stroke is fired double-action. The trigger both cocks and fires the handgun by trigger action. The slide does not cock the hammer, but rather the hammer rides down with the slide

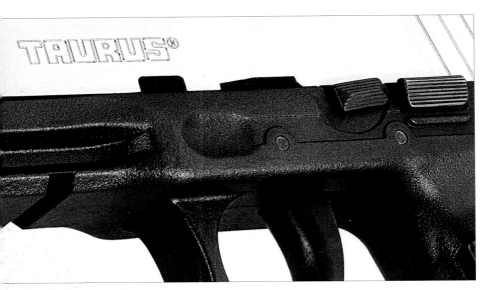

When familiarizing yourself with the various slide locks and safety levers of the handgun, be certain that you know which lever is for takedown and which is for the slide lock. Basic gunhandling demands this familiarity. *Taurus*

but does not fire the pistol. A double-action press is the only trigger action to learn. As a rule, the DAO trigger is midway between the position of a single-action and a double-action trigger when at rest and features a shorter stroke than the standard double-action pistol. SIG has mastered the art with the new SIG P250 pistol, a smooth and manageable DAO-type handgun.

The Glock system bears some discussion. When the slide of the Glock is racked, the striker or firing pin is moved to a partially cocked position. It is held against spring pressure. The Glock trigger is pressed and supplies the necessary movement to completely depress the striker against spring pressure. The sear falls away from the contact point with the striker, and the striker runs forward and fires the pistol. The action is repeated for subsequent shots.

The Glock is classed by the regulating authority as a double-action–only handgun, and that is what it is. The Glock is an easy action to learn. While a DAO pistol may not give the crisp let off of a well tuned single-action, training time is drastically reduced as compared to the double-action pistol with a decocker. Whether reducing training time is a respectable goal or not, it is the goal of the bean counters.

FEED AND CYCLE RELIABILITY

Most automatics feature a controlled feed. The cartridge is inserted into the magazine. The follower is depressed and the cartridges are slipped under the magazine feed lips until the magazine is full. The feed lips capture the cartridge, and the magazine spring keeps the rounds in place. When the slide is racked, the

The fixed-barrel Makarov features a safety that works the opposite of most double-action pistols. The safety is up for on and down for off safe, the opposite of the Beretta and Smith Wesson.

cocking block moves a cartridge forward into the chamber. Often, the bullet nose is stopped slightly on the feed ramp and is snugged into the breech face. This is often true with Browning and Colt pistols. The Beretta M9, on the other hand, feeds the cartridge practically straight into the chamber.

Cycle reliability means the pistol is reliable with a certain type of ammunition. As an example, some .22-caliber target pistols are reliable only with high-velocity ammunition. Others will function with standard-velocity target ammunition. The German Luger demands full-power 9mm Luger ammunition. Some handguns will function with a wide variety of loads from target-grade loadings to powerful +P loadings. Be certain to confirm the feed and cycle reliability of your particular handgun.

Let's look at the manual of arms for each type of self-loader. The manual of arms is simply the standard operating procedure for each handgun type. The manual of

Single-action handgun, Browning High Power or Colt 1911

Load

Place safety on

Holster

Draw

Disengage safety

Fire

Double-action first-shot handgun

Load

Decock

Holster

Draw

Fire

Double-action first-shot handgun with a safety

Load

Decock; leave safety in the on position

Holster

Draw

Disengage safety

Fire

Selective double-action handgun

Load

Lower the hammer manually

Holster

Draw

Fire

Double-action–only handgun

Load

Holster

Draw

Fire

arms (chart at left) assumes you are preparing to carry the handgun for serious purposes. The manual of arms gives instructions on making the piece ready for carry and on firing the handgun. A less complicated handgun may appeal to you, but many handgunners prefer the single-action automatic with a safety. Remember, when beginning to master the handgun, load it only on the firing range.

CHAPTER 8

Safety

IF YOU TAKE ONLY ONE chapter in this book to heart, make it this one. Safety rules cannot be enforced strictly enough. Vehicle and gun safety have much in common, save for an inescapable fact. The public holds each handgunner responsible for the actions of the other. It isn't fair, but it is a fact. A drunk driver may not reflect badly on the rest of the driving populace, but let someone have a range accident and the public is ready to close the range down for good. That being said, let's look at the aspects of handgun safety.

There are two separate concerns, actually, and that is range safety and personal handgun safety. Everyone wishes to be the high-speed low-drag operator. It takes a lot of work and discipline to get there. You have to begin somewhere. Safety is that place of departure. Only when you are a safe and conscientious gunhandler will you be taken seriously as a handgunner. Firearms are a fact of life in my house. We also use chainsaws, the occasional torch, and then there are the Jeeps. None will suffer fools. When you attend a range, be it public or private, there is nothing in the construction that will keep you safe without your adherence to safety rules. The human element is always the weakest link.

Some procedures work better than others and each range will have a carefully written document that explains the safety rules. Adherence to these rules is essential. There are universal rules for every range and specific rules for individual ranges. A good beginning is to

No matter what the circumstances, when you are holding a handgun the trigger finger should be out of the trigger guard and alongside the frame, not on the trigger.

be certain that all firearms are unloaded and the actions locked open during transit to the range. The actions remain open until you reach the firing line. This means the cylinder of a revolver is open and the slide is locked to the rear in the case of the self-loading pistol. The handguns are not loaded until you are ready to fire. At this point you should have your hearing protection and sturdy range glasses on. If you are near other people, be certain that all is ready on the line and that the other shooters have their glasses on. Be certain no one has traveled downrange to change targets. The command "Ready on the line!" is normally given before firing.

A rule that is vital is that all rounds be fired downrange. Even if you have a large protecting berm on each side, fire every round downrange. In the none too distant past many ranges, particularly police ranges, were comprised of a single wide firing line with a high berm behind the target frames. Shooters fired more or less abreast of the other. Today ranges are more often portioned with high berms separating the range sections, and indoor ranges often have bulletproof constructs between the firing lanes. I recall police qualifications with points of fire ranging from seven to fifty yards. With a moving line of cops we had to be careful and realize what the man on your left or right was doing.

The author is demonstrating holster safety. The finger is alongside the holster, not in the trigger guard. This step will avoid holster-related discharges.

There is always a level of danger in police and military training, but it is rigidly controlled. An important point is to maintain a correct distance from steel targets. Steel reaction targets are a great training aid, but bullet fragments may bounce back nearly to the shooter if you are not careful. Ten yards is a realistic minimum range of engagement.

Be certain that your bullets are directed into the target. I have seen twenty-foot-tall pine trees on the hill behind the berm in police training take a beating. Target discipline is important. Always fire for the center of the target and use an appropriate target stand. Firing at rocks and other bric-a-brac on the ground is tempting but may result in a ricochet. A glancing shot's direction is unpredictable. You will be expelled from the range for such behavior. Range safety is comprised primarily of properly directing your shots and maintaining muzzle discipline; the muzzle is always pointed downrange. Be aware of others on the range and use proper targets. A rule I feel is important will save you heartache at a later date: Keep only one handgun and type of ammunition on the shooting bench at one time. I have seen 9mm cartridges fired in .40-caliber chambers, often with a blown case head. Other mismatches would be a disaster.

Under the tutelage of an NRA-certified instructor these students are attending a basic class. Note that their revolvers are in the safe condition with the cylinders open.

HANDLING THE PISTOL

How you handle the pistol determines safety not only on the range but at home. Tactical doctrine is important, but the first lesson should be concerning safety. We do not wish to be the police officer who admitted he was in four and a half gunfights. The half of a gunfight came when he shot himself in the leg. Before you become a tactical shooter or a handgun hunter you must learn safety and keep safety first at all times. Handguns are potentially lethal and must be respected. A responsible shooter presents himself to the public in this manner and will not be labeled a dangerous person. You must follow safety rules even when under the stress of a pistol match or when handling a handgun in a hurry to get off a shot at a fine game animal.

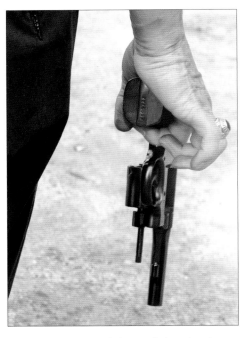

This very experienced shooter is keeping the cylinder of his Combat Masterpiece .38 open during an NRA basic handgun class. There is no other way to conduct yourself!

Safety rules exist for public and private property. I have seen as many as a dozen rules posted at ranges, but I think we may easily condense these rules to only four; however, they are four very important rules.

RULE 1

All Guns Are Always Loaded

By checking and verifying the state of the handgun and remaining in control of our handgun and its state of readiness, we are safer in every way. We know whether the piece is loaded or unloaded, but we will check again every time the handgun changes hands. We do so by opening the action, checking visually, and with our finger in the chamber or cylinder as well. There is only one way and that is the right way.

RULE 2

Never Let the Muzzle Cover Anything You Are Not Willing to Destroy

This is an obvious piece of wisdom that will avoid practically every handgun accident. A handgun is short. It is easy to allow the muzzle to cover your own body. You must always know exactly where the muzzle is pointed, and it should

This young military intelligence officer knows that the only safe way to begin a class is by checking the magazine and chamber of the Browning 9mm he is handling.

never be pointed toward your body or in the direction of another person. Within the year, adherence to this rule has saved the author much trouble. On the first occasion I was checking out a rather nice example of an early-model Astra handgun. I loaded the magazine with CCI/Speer Blazer ammunition in 9mm Largo caliber. When I racked the slide, the pistol fired and raised a cloud of dust in front of the shooting bench. I had not caught the fact that the firing pin was stuck forward from varnished powder. When the slide was racked the pistol fired.

On another occasion I had finished a practice session with a new pistol. I had been carrying the piece and as I prepared to leave the private range I elected to load and holster the pistol. I loaded the magazine into the frame, racked the slide, and

Note the tall berm behind the target. When testing ammunition, the author follows all safety rules. Note that the line of flight of the bullet is angled slightly downward.

Many modern tactical pistols feature forward-cocking serrations. While fine for tactical use, the serrations are mounted at the rear of the slide as a matter of course. Your hands will be far from the muzzle.

pressed the decocker. When the hammer fell, the pistol fired. This is the only time I have suffered a decocker failure in forty years of shooting. What had happened was that particles of brass had been blown under the firing pin block and the firing block or drop safety was stuck in the fire position.

In this particular design the hammer actually strikes the firing pin during the decock, but the firing pin block keeps the pistol from firing. I much prefer the SIG system, which lowers the hammer to a place just short of the firing pin. In this particular instance, I was glad that my training had been so firmly followed that the pistol was pointed toward the earth. Control that muzzle!

RULE 3
Keep Your Finger Off of the Trigger Until You Fire

This does not mean when you think you will fire or when you are about to fire but when you fire. Your sights will be on the target and you are beginning the trigger press. Placing the finger on register before this moment or during movement is the mark of a duffer. If you fall, you will jerk the trigger. You may shoot yourself or your partner.

RULE 4
Be Certain of Your Target

Always positively identify the target. Otherwise you are subjecting all involved to a ricochet. Be certain that the target you have set up is protected by an adequate backstop, no matter where the bullet strikes on the target. Dry fire is an essential skill that may be practiced at home. The target you are dry firing against is real. You cannot regard it any other way. Be certain when dry firing that the target you are dry firing against will stop a bullet from the handgun you are firing.

GUNHANDLING

Gunhandling is distinct from marksmanship. You need to cultivate the ability to think a few seconds ahead and consider what could happen if you mishandle the handgun. When the handgun is difficult to break open or resists an attempt at unloading, then the stakes are higher and your utmost attention is demanded. A bit of unburned powder or a defect in the cartridge—however rare—may be at play. Safety comes first, and the occasional refresher is well advised.

To look back at our safety rules I believe that the single most important ingredient of safety is to keep your finger off of the trigger until you fire. You may keep the finger on the frame alongside of the trigger guard

The author's well worn Springfield LW .45, top, is in the ready position, cocked and locked, hammer to the rear and safety on. The Walther P1 9mm, below, is locked open. There is no question the lower pistol is unloaded.

with no loss in speed during competition or any other pursuit. As you address the sight picture, move the trigger finger to the face of the trigger and begin the trigger

The author appreciates the fact that the cocked-and-locked 1911 features a locked hammer and trigger when properly carried with the slide lock safety on. Just the same, he is always diligent when holstering the handgun.

press. If you fall with the finger in register on the trigger face, there is almost a certainty of an accident discharge. One hand's fingers tighten in concert with the other, and if the weak hand grabs something for support, the firing hand's finger will also tighten. This is part of being the physically symmetrical creations we are, that our two sides mirror each other at all times.

CHILDREN AND FIREARMS

The question often comes up as to what age a child should be when introduced to firearms. I was young but went hunting with my grandfather and learned the rules of safety. The child's behavior and general level of self-discipline are most important. A disobedient child will not rise to a higher level of maturity at the range. If the child is respectful and listens well and is obedient in all other matters, then they are ready for indoctrination in safety first and then the shooting skills. A disrespectful child, or unreasonable adult, has no business on the firing range. Children have a curiosity about firearms that may be to their benefit or to their ruin. The responsible adult must lead them in the right direction.

HOLSTER SAFETY

When you advance to live fire on the range and drawing a loaded handgun from the holster, holster safety must be rigidly respected. This is also true of competition, hunting, or personal defense. You will holster a loaded handgun, draw the

This young instructor is teaching an all-military class. Even with such excellent human resources, safety is always the first concern.

The SIG features a well designed decocker. The frame-mounted decocker may be activated without disturbing the firing grip and should always be used rather than lowering the hammer manually.

handgun, and fire and reholster the handgun. You must take care when holstering the handgun that the trigger does not contact the holster lip.

There is a possibility that the trigger will contact the holster and fire the handgun. A common accidental discharge with the police handgun is when the handgun is holstered and the safety strap or thumb break comes into contact with the trigger and fires the handgun. To avoid this problem, angle the handgun into the holster from the rear and let the muzzle move into the holster underneath the safety strap and angle the barrel into the holster. Holstering problems most often occur when the handgun is holstered with the trigger finger held in the trigger guard. This is a common mistake that will surely fire the handgun as the pistol is holstered.

The proper means of making certain the pistol is safe is to open the cylinder of the revolver and lock the slide to the rear with the pistol. There is no question as to whether the handgun is loaded.

CHAPTER 9

Marksmanship

HANDGUN MARKSMANSHIP IS CHALLENGING. I will not sugarcoat anything for you. Mastering the handgun is more difficult than mastering the rifle or shotgun. Just the same, it is not impossible, certainly not as challenging as becoming a maestro of the violin or mastering the great Kentucky finger-picking guitar style ala Merle Travis.

The psycho motor reality is there; you simply have to realize that errors come from pushing the shot. In other words, we walk before we can crawl. We are not reinventing the wheel; we are simply going with acceptable doctrine that works. There are preparatory steps we take before traveling to the firing range and progressive instructional tips. The fundamentals or basics of handgun marksmanship are a pyramid, with the grip, aim, breath control, trigger compression, and target engagement covered in ever more detail as we progress. It is most important to learn the right way first. Once bad habits are ingrained, the shooter will have difficulty shedding these habits.

I prefer a student that is a *tabula rasa*, a blank slate. If you have preconceived notions that are incorrect, learn to shoot in the proper manner. Leave bad habits behind once they are discovered. Be open to attempting techniques that may feel strange at first. I assure you they will be profitable.

Even an old Luger can be coached into good accuracy. Note that two of the bullet holes show two shots in one hole. Fiocchi JSP loads were used in this .30 Luger. With better trigger control, the group would be even tighter.

EYE DOMINANCE

Quite a few shooters impede their progress by failing to discern which is their dominant eye. We have less difficulty in determining which is the dominant hand, as we all live either with the right hand or the left hand dominant. There is much involved in left- or right-brain dominance. If you are right handed and have a left dominant eye, do not despair. Many of the finest competition shots have fired with the left eye crossing over to the sights. Often, the less dominant eye is strong enough for pistol shooting in any case. Just the same, it is profitable to understand which eye is the dominant eye. With both eyes open, focus on a small object such as a light switch panel about twelve to fourteen feet from the eye. Extend both arms and hands at full extension and then bring the hands to meet, with a triangle-shaped opening between the thumbs. Place the object in view in the center of this opening in the hands. Focus until the object is clear. Then close one eye or the other. You may need to bring the hands closer, but at some point you will close one eye and the object will not be visible. When you close one eye and the object remains visible, that is the dominant eye.

The proper sight picture and sight alignment is important. These custom-grade sights are factory supplied with the Taurus 24/7 and offer an ideal all-around sight picture. *Taurus*

GRIPPING THE HANDGUN

The grip is essential to holding the handgun properly as we fire. To achieve a good grip the hand wraps around the handle and the fingers are wrapped around the front strap, with the three fingers on the front strap exerting equal pressure to the rear. To find the correct pressure of the grip, squeeze the grip until your hand trembles, then back off. You have found the proper grip. The pressure of the fingers must be equal and the fingers cannot move when the trigger finger exerts pressure on the trigger.

The proper grip is essential for trigger control, recoil control, and follow through. The hand slides on to the grip with the thumb and forefinger open in a Y. The hand should be high on the back strap. The modern double-action revolver and modern self-loading pistols feature a grip strap that stabilizes the hand. With the single-action revolver more study is needed, but the hand should be placed high on the grip in order for the trigger finger to reach forward and properly control the trigger. This is the ideal grip placement.

For the two-hand hold, wrap the support hand around the firing hand. The forefinger of the support hand should be wrapped around the third finger of the firing hand with the fingers of the firing hand curled into the heel of the support hand. Some favor the competitor's grip, which places most of the gripping strength in the support hand and perhaps forty percent in the firing hand. This makes a comfortable relaxed grip in firing long strings during competition. For personal defense and taking an important shot in hunting, a proper strong grip is always desirable.

Sometimes a long firing session with a powerful handgun requires shooting gloves. PAST is among the best. Midwa shooting supply offers many such products. *MidwayUSA*

There are several thumb positions shooters like to use. As a rule, the strong thumbs-forward grip, with the thumbs not interlocked but the shooting hand thumb laying over the weak hand thumb, is the best grip. This grip works well with all self-loaders, but if you attempt this grip with the revolver the thumb may interfere with the rotating cylinder of the revolver. It depends upon the size of the thumbs and the exact model of revolver, but in all cases be certain that your grip does not interfere with the action of the revolver. The thumbs must not ride on the controls of the self-loader. During recoil, it is possible for the nonfiring hand to bump into the magazine release or slide lock if the grip is not properly maintained. The grip must be consistently applied for good results, and in the case of the automatic pistol, in order for the pistol to function properly.

FIRING WITH ONE HAND

In classic bull's-eye competition, only one hand is used. After all, the handgun is often referred to as the one-hand gun. I have known many shooters who for one reason or another did not have the use of both hands. There is no reason you cannot become a proficient shot with one hand with the one-hand gun.

Personal-defense shooters should be proficient with one-hand fire at close range as well. The classic bull's-eye stance is taken with the body bladed to the target. The strong side arm is extended along with the strong side foot, with the weak side foot to the rear. The classic thumb hooked in the belt stance is popular, but I have seen shooters tuck the weak side hand in the pocket as well. Whatever is

This shooter has fired a good group by any standards. Fired at short range, this group with the .32 ACP and Winchester ammunition shows good control.

comfortable works. Some face the target, others do not blade the body as severely as others. Whichever stance you take it is important that the foot position is one in which the weight of the body is evenly distributed and the position is comfortable during long firing strings. Most of the weight of the body is on the forward leg. With some practice this stance will become second nature and you will notice your proficiency climbing with each practice round.

Personal-defense one-hand shooting may require that you learn to control recoil but bull-s-eye shooting does not. You will be firing the .22 or a .45 with a lighter recoiling target load. As such, the one-hand hold will help the shooter master the basics of accurate shot placement without the problems of recoil. Just the same, the longer the range the more challenging the one-hand stance and proper control will become.

AIMING THE HANDGUN

When you aim the handgun you guide the bullet. There is no mysterious martial art involved and no technique involved that will guide the bullet without the use of the sights. The bottom line is that you wish the point of impact on the target to be controlled by the point of aim of the sights. There are many types of handgun sights but all rely on the same principle. Some sights are snag free for use in concealed-carry handguns; some are quite high profile for target shooting. Hunting handgun sights are often fully adjustable. All require the same alignment.

There are two important steps in aiming. While a trained shooter may do both simultaneously they are separate and one comes before the other. The first is sight alignment. When sight alignment is addressed, the front post is centered in the rear sight notch. The top of the notch is perfectly aligned with the top of the rear sights. Sight picture is the imposition of the sights on the target. The sights are aligned properly, which you can see, and the sights are then aligned on the target with the front post just under the place on the target you wish to hit with the bullet. The most common sight picture is the six o'clock hold with the front sight under the bull. Some prefer to center the front post on the target. When the sights are fully adjustable the chore is much easier.

Modern firearms are sometimes perfectly sighted for one bullet weight or the other, sometimes not, but do not adjust the sights until you are making good groups on the paper. The focus should be on the front sight. The front sight must be clear and sharp. The target may be allowed to blur. Remember, error in sighting is more important than having a perfect focus on the target. If you make a 1/10-inch error in sighting, the bullet will impact fifteen inches off target at twenty-five yards. This is a magnification of 150 times.

This shooter is demonstrating good form at moderate range. Note the brightly colored target and good backstop.

BREATH CONTROL

Those of you who have mastered the martial arts, particularly karate, understand the vital aspects of breath control. When you are breathing, your body is constantly moving. Holding your breath is not acceptable, but learning to break the shot at the proper moment is vital.

In target shooting you take normal breaths, releasing about half of the air in the lungs, then hold your breath for the momentary time needed to break the shot.

This shooter shows ideal form with the one hand grip. The trigger finger is in the proper position and so is the thumb.

This is practically the ideal shooting grip with the Ruger .22. Note that both thumbs are pointed forward.

The maximized benefit occurs a few seconds after the breath is held. The shooter then finishes exhaling, takes a breath, and begins again.

TIP

When beginning to learn pistol marksmanship, you may find that you tremble with fatigue after firing. Be certain to take a break from time to time. You are using arm and shoulder muscles you have never used in quite this way. By the same token, if you experience eyestrain, stare into the distance with no particular focus and let your eyes reach their natural focus point. Do this for a few minutes, and you will find that you are able to pick back up where you left off and resume firing as accurately as before.

TRIGGERNOMETRY

I don't know who coined the term "triggernometry" as a play on trigger control and geometry, but they hit the bull's-eye with that one. There is a certain amount of geometry at play. Trigger control is vital. If you do not have a perfect sight picture

When firing a handgun with heavy recoil, a good grip and firing stance are essential. This shooter is using the Weaver stance to control the exuberant recoil of an HK .45.

you will hit the target somewhere. If you do not control the grip properly, your shots will not be smoothly delivered. If you jerk the trigger, then you will miss by the proverbial mile.

You must learn to control the trigger press while not allowing the sights to waver. When pressing the trigger the trigger finger compresses it, resulting in the trigger loosing the sear, which connects the trigger to the hammer and firing the handgun. A surprise break is desirable. You compress the trigger until the action breaks, and you should not know the exact moment when it breaks. Some try to ambush the trigger and jerk the action. This is a killer to accuracy. Others will attempt to control the trigger action, realize they are running out of time to break the shot, and quickly press the trigger. This results in a miss.

The shooter will anticipate the shot and sometimes the muscles will tense up in anticipation of recoil. You cannot allow this to happen. Trigger control is so important I have devoted the final section of this report to trigger control. Remember, the slow press used in bull's-eye may not be applicable to combat shooting, but the same control is exercised. You gradually break the shot. In rapid-fire competition, you simply fire more rapidly with a greater emphasis on speed. You are using faster compressions but not quick ones, not jerks of the trigger.

Begin with placing the first joint of the trigger finger directly on the trigger face.

Trigger compression must be straight to the rear. Do not speed up and miss! Flinching or recoil anticipation is ruinous to accuracy, as the hand will involuntarily jerk before the hammer falls. A surprise break aids in controlling flinch. Another

In this illustration, the author is using a stance that is sometimes called the modified Weaver. The good elements of the Weaver are maintained, but the shooter is not bladed quite as sharply.

The Weaver is often modified to allow peace officers to present the bulletproof vest to the target rather than the open side of the vest when the shooter is sharply bladed. The author is demonstrating with a rare pistol, the SIG P220 in .38 ACP Super.

aid in follow-through is not to release the trigger too quickly. This is especially important in mastering a double-action handgun, particularly the double-action revolver. The trigger is pressed and allowed to reset. The time involved in firing and allowing the reset is as close to the same as possible. This allows great control and greater accuracy.

FOLLOW-THROUGH

Follow-through is important in many sports and particularly in handgunning. We mentioned follow-through with the trigger. Follow-through is also important with the firing grip. Follow-through in its essential form is a nondeviation from the shooting stance and grip. Moving the body, shifting the grip, or other movement is detrimental to accuracy. Accuracy is delivering the shot to the same place on demand. If you miss the target with the first shot, the second will be off as well and the result is a general degradation of accuracy. Even if the sights need adjustment, by firing consistently you will produce a good group and know that you are achieving a goal.

Follow-through is essential because in some cases the handgun is recoiling while the bullet is still in the barrel. If you do not maintain a consistent hold the point of impact will be all over the target. All of the basics must come together in firing a shot. If you are off in one or the other the result is a miss.

CALLING THE SHOT

You should develop the ability to call the shot. You should know whether or not the shot you just fired was a hit. If you jerked the trigger you will miss. If you moved the sights, you will miss. You need to develop the ability to call your shots and realize whether or not you have hit the target.

SHOOTING STANCES

We have mentioned foot position and a comfortable, solid shooting stance. During the beginning of your shooting experience balance is important. You may also wish to learn to shoot from a bench rest. While bench rest shooting is practical, primarily for firing in order to sight the handgun, it is also a good means of eliminating

This shooter has practiced a great deal with the handgun, beginning at a very young age. The locked thumbs and wrap-around two-hand grip are perfectly executed.

many variables. As you advance there will be times when you will wish to adopt the bench rest position to fire and determine the accuracy of a certain handgun or handgun ammunition. Bench resting is necessary to sight the handgun, so you must learn to properly control the handgun off of the rest.

OFF-HAND SHOOTING

The isosceles might have been called the triangular stance, but the system is simple. The feet are about a yard apart and the arms are thrust forward with the handgun at eye level. It is that simple.

Be careful to not let the head sag to the arm, but rather keep the handgun up at eye level and your head erect. The trunk is bent only slightly forward from the hips with the isosceles, not the over-done stance we sometimes see. The weaver stance is more complicated but affords greater stability. The body is bladed to the target and both elbows are bent. The strong side hand is a full-length extension, while the support hand reaches for the strong side hand and brings it slightly rearward with both elbows bent to allow flex and recoil absorption. Coupled with a boxer's stance, the Weaver stance gives unprecedented stability.

This shooter is practicing with the Taurus M44 .44 Magnum. She is using her favorite firing stance, the isosceles. It works for her and that is what counts.

MORE ON TRIGGER CONTROL

Some handguns have heavier actions than others, but a good shooter will be trained to use the trigger he has. Whether the target is a bull's-eye pulp paper target or a steel gong or the vitals of a game animal, trigger control is everything. All the fundaments are taken in measure, but leave mastering the trigger out of this equation and you will have as much fun as a person riding through a briar patch while wearing shorts. Jerking the trigger is the most detrimental single problem that my students have. The answer is this: You must cause the hammer to fall without disturbing the sight picture.

Some triggers are as crisp as we prefer. This means the trigger breaks cleanly without excess creep. Creep is that unpleasant motion that indicates that the trigger is moving inconsistently. Backlash is felt after the hammer drops. Neither is for the best, but either may be handled by a good marksman. Some like smooth trigger faces and others thin triggers, and some like serrated triggers. Work with what you have until you master the handgun in question, then look further. The best means of mastering the trigger may be done in the home.

DRY FIRE

Dry fire is simply pressing and practicing the trigger without live ammunition. Safety must be followed. Use a triple-checked unloaded handgun. Always notify everyone in the home you are dry firing. In my home we all check the firearm. Finally, be certain that you are dry firing toward a place that is not normally a point of human travel. Do not aim at a spot in the study if the den is on the other side. Your aiming point should be finite, always used, and offer a good backstop. If you are using a .22, a stack of books would stop a bullet just in case. (I will not go into stories that illustrate the obvious, but there is no shortage of such episodes.) If you are dry firing a .357 Magnum you need more back stop. This is an incontrovertible safety measure.

Take care to hold the pistol properly. Take a good sight picture and practice sight alignment. Keep the grip steady. Dry fire is about as tiring as live fire and will build the muscles used in firing the handgun. I have seen old-time handgunners place a dime on the top of a revolver's front sight and cycle the revolver repeatedly with the dime balanced on the front sight. I have done it myself. Defects in trigger control will make themselves known as you practice dry fire in the home. There are differences in each action in regards to trigger control. As an example, when the trigger of a double-action handgun is pressed through the long arc, sometimes the little finger moves in sympathetic reaction. This must be noticed and taken care of. Some attempt to stage the trigger of a double-action, bringing the hammer almost to the breaking point, taking an aim, and then firing. It doesn't work. Even those who use this technique and seem to be doing well will do better work with a straight-through trigger press.

When you press the trigger, you will move the sights if you do not control the trigger. Dry fire is the best road to proficiency with any type of handgun. Take your time, press slowly, and wait for the surprise break. We are not surprised the handgun is going to fire, but the momentary break, not a jerky action, is what we wish to achieve. Even when you move to a faster press and a string of shots you will be managing each shot quickly but carefully.

AN ANALYSIS OF ABILITY THROUGH SHOT GROUPING

A great aid in trigger control is the ability to call your shots. Common problems causing a miss include rolling the trigger finger inward, tightening the entire hand on firing, applying pressure with both thumbs, and canting the firearm to the left or the right.

READING A TARGET

If the shots are high, then you may be pushing with the heel of the hand. You may be anticipating recoil and flinching upwards.

If the shots are to the left you may be rolling the trigger finger inwards. You may be flexing the firing hand.

If the shots are to the right, you may be rolling the trigger finger inwards if you are left handed. You may be milking the trigger in a milking motion or canting the handgun in the wrong direction.

LOW SHOTS

You may be pushing forward with the gripping hand. You may have poor wrist lock or the proverbial limp writing that is ruinous to accuracy. Flinching downwards or anticipating recoil also results in low shots.

CHAPTER 10

The First Handgun

I RECEIVE MANY INQUIRIES CONCERNING THE first handgun. A long-distance diagnoses isn't ideal, but I have developed a take-two-aspirins-and-call-me-in-the-morning approach. I have learned to be patient and I hope I am not a doctrinaire. Those of us who have managed to become accomplished handgunners often use the terms "novice" or "beginner" for first-time shooters. I find the term "rookie" obnoxious, and we have to remember we were all rank beginners at one time.

When learning a different discipline or a different handgun we often revert to these beginnings. Some who purchase the first handgun have some prior shooting experience, but others do not. There are various degrees of expertise encountered. I think that the best course is to regard beginners as people who have never owned a handgun even if they have fired a handgun.

These Rugers are customized with special grips to suit each shooter. Top to bottom are grips from Pachmayr, the factory Ruger, and finally a set of grips from Hogue.

The reasons for interest in handguns are many. These days, the majority of new shooters are interested in personal defense. A few are interested in hunting and some are interested in competition. Quite a few are simply curious. People who are interested in antique watches, steam engines, aircraft, and history will often become interested in handguns. Once they are exposed to handguns some become avid shooters while others become accumulators or collectors. It is the same interest that some have in a finely made product of historical interest.

Handguns that are not the best choice to learn marksmanship or handgunning with will distract the shooter. As an example, the North American .22-caliber Mini Revolver is a niche handgun that is good to have but not well suited to a beginner. The same may be said of the .44 Magnum revolver. This is despite the fact that such a handgun may be ideally suited to the novice's particular situation. The point is, while your pursuits may indicate one choice, if you have no experience you may need to start elsewhere. A beginner cannot rely on skills they cannot demonstrate. I know folks who should be carrying a .357 Magnum revolver or a .45 Commander, but neither is a handgun for beginners. Quality firearms are not inexpensive. Proficiency at arms is purchased with a different coin. You need to begin with a handgun that builds skill rather than defeats the shooter.

The first handgun should be a basic handgun that is simple to operate. An inexpensive handgun is okay but not a cheap handgun. Pride of ownership and good function are encouraging aspects of the handgunning game. A poorly made or troublesome handgun will discourage the shooter. Many first-time shooters

There is no better first self-loading handgun available than the Ruger Standard Model .22. There are target-grade variations, long-barrel versions, and even a polymer-frame pistol.

move up a notch in quality soon after the initial purchase to a handgun better suited to their needs. Others find handguns interesting and realize that more than one handgun is needed to fulfill their interest or needs. We often come to own handguns we would never deploy for serious use but which we find interesting. The Webley revolvers are examples of these.

The inexpensive Nagant revolvers and the CZ 52 are interesting but not something the beginning should try, although they are popular first handguns because they are so inexpensive. The Nagant in particular would convince a newbie that handguns are impossibly difficult to use well, inaccurate, and unwieldy. An overly complicated handgun or one for which ammunition is difficult to find causes the first-time shooter to be filled with buyer's remorse. Surplus pistols are seldom useful as primary handguns and are not true collector's gems but rather they are special-interest handguns.

If the person looking for a first handgun has a long-term goal of becoming a handgun hunter, then the .44 Magnum isn't the first choice. They should work up in increments. The Ruger Single Six .22-caliber revolver is the new plus-ultra of single-action handguns. As a bonus you will never outgrow this handgun. It will give good service for decades, take small game, and provide hours of recreation, even after you acquire your .357 or .44 revolver. Some shooters move seamlessly up the ladder to single-action automatics and the Magnum revolvers; others progress more slowly.

We must pay our dues with the first handgun. A good swing-out cylinder double-action revolver is still the best first choice for a first handgun no matter what type of handgun you envision working up to. The action is easily learned,

Jenny Graff, a feature writer for *Belle Magazine*, is preparing to fire her first shot with a handgun. She was excited but also had some trepidation.

A beginning handgun should have a well balanced feel, a heavy barrel, and good-sized bold sights. The Taurus Tracker .22 has all of this.

Jenny Graff is carefully loading the Taurus Tracker .22. There is simply nothing as well suited to early training as the double-action revolver.

After the initial indoctrination Graff fired her first rounds from a Smith & Wesson center-fire revolver. She did well.

accuracy is good, and the revolver is accurate enough for practice to be interesting. There is no need to begin with a .22 automatic if you are meaning to adopt a center-fire automatic at a later date. The .22 automatic, after all, doesn't have a lot in common with a 9mm automatic. I have observed shooters who were completely frustrated by malfunctions with automatic pistols. You must learn to load the pistol properly and grip it consistently. The revolver is not as racy as the automatic, but it is functional and accuracy is excellent with the best quality examples.

The inexpensive and inoffensive .22-rimfire cartridge has many advantages. Low recoil and inexpensive ammunition are the primary advantages. A good choice for beginners is the Taurus Tracker revolver. The Tracker has comfortable "ribber" grips that fit most hands well. The double-action is smooth enough for meaningful practice, the single-action trigger is crisp, and the revolver has an overall modern look that is appealing. A shooter who makes a poor choice in the initial purchase often corrects the mistake by moving to a higher quality handgun while taking a beating on the trade in of his clunker.

The Taurus Tracker will suit your needs and not be outgrown. A desire for more features, more power, or a superior defensive handgun will motivate the move to a larger or more powerful handgun than the Tracker .22. If you strongly prefer a .22-caliber automatic pistol, the Ruger Standard Model or the Browning Buckmark are good choices. For the shooter who prefers a self-loader, either is a great pick. I own both and would be hard pressed to choose which one I prefer. Sometimes you may wish to adopt a rim fire that is similar to the center fire you aspire to master. As an example, the Ruger .22/45 is similar to the 1911 pistol as far as the control layout goes. Even the grip frame is similar. The SIG Mosquito is a downsized rimfire version of the P Series. When we are wrestling with the big bores, it is always nice to come back to the .22 and leave behind the distractions of flash blast and recoil. A good .22 is a lifetime investment.

When it comes to quality there are many choices, but when you purchase Smith & Wesson, Browning, Ruger, and Taurus you are paying for more than the name. You are paying for proven performance. A good rule for satisfaction is to choose a middle-of-the-road handgun with features that place it squarely in the middle of the price line. Spending too much or too little at this stage of the game is counterproductive.

Some folks wish to go ahead and get a good-quality defensive handgun with the first handgun and skip the .22. With dedication to training this may work just fine. Most shooters will choose either a 9mm automatic or a .38 revolver. These

This is a special model of the Ruger Standard Model. Note the red dot sight and Hogue custom grips. A simpler handgun may be best for the beginner, but this is a fun handgun.

are the largest calibers the average shooter will care to begin with and in truth the largest calibers that we will master with a minimum of experience. A double-action revolver or a double-action first-shot handgun is a good choice.

My friend Matthew Bishop began shooting with a Ruger P89 9mm. My friend Lee Bishop began with an H and K 9mm. Although both went to the .45 at a later date, their time with the 9mm was well spent. Both realized at a later date they really needed a good .22 for all around shooting. But the 9mm remains a good first

It is important that the handgun fit the hand well, which is why Pachmayr and Hogue grips are so popular. The author prefers the Hogue on lighter guns, while the Pachmayr is his favorite on target-weight pistols.

This is the polymer frame Ruger .22/45. The pistol is similar to the 1911 in layout, but this handgun is well capable of standing on its own merits.

choice. With quality ammunition such as the Black Hills "blue box" line available on the cheap, shooting is affordable. A good-quality automatic is accurate enough for meaningful practice. If you are among the shooters who prefer the revolver the Taurus 82 is among the best choices. I prefer a revolver with adjustable sights, although many shooters prefer rugged fixed sights. If the revolver shoots to the point of aim with a standard weight bullet, that is fine, but if not some adjustment is needed. A medium-frame six-shot .38 or .357 revolver is ideal. (Load the .357 with .38 loads in the beginning.)

A few words on the revolver: After a recent class in which a couple of the students were, let's say, harrowing, an instructor remarked that some people have no business with an automatic pistol. He has a valid point. It is amazing that the less dedicated shooters not willing to listen to proven doctrine often show up with a difficult-to-handle handgun. The revolver is an ideal beginners handgun. On the other hand, I have started from scratch at a police department and got officers up and running and qualified in one day. It isn't easy, but we have done it. Even today much of the police training in America is done on a crisis basis.

HANDFIT

When you choose a first handgun, handfit is critical. You take the handgun in your hand at the shop and make certain the pistol is comfortable to hold. The digits of your hand must not be over stretched when reaching for the trigger or controls. To evaluate handfit, take the handgun in one hand and be certain that the bones of the hand are lined up behind the axis or bore line of the handgun. The hand should be comfortable at the top of the grip strap, and none of the fingers should hang over the bottom of the grip. (A few handguns such as the original Single Action Army are cramped for the average hand. We live with them.)

The trigger finger should comfortably reach to the face of the trigger. Some handguns are too much of a reach for average-size hands. The polymer-frame double-action–only handguns in the big-bore calibers are perhaps the worst offenders. These handguns may force you to use the H grip or cocked to one side

For the beginner needing a good defense handgun right now, the double-action revolver is a great choice. This Smith & Wesson .357 Magnum revolver is carried in a Tucker pancake holster. This is good kit all the way around.

Small carry guns firing powerful cartridges are too specialized for the beginner. They may prove daunting and may even impede progress.

grip. This is ruinous to accuracy. If the forefinger does not have proper leverage you will not be able to control the trigger. A handgun with a good fit and feel is essential for good shooting. The Glock Model 17, SIG P series, the Taurus 24/7, and the Colt 1911 are among the best choices. In revolvers the K-frame or medium-frame revolvers are ideal. The .44 and .45-frame revolvers are more specialized and, while useful for deliberate fire in hunting, are overall slow to handle. Even if you are able to handle a large-frame handgun on the range, when you are in the field with sweaty hands or in a retention situation, control is much more difficult.

I have covered the important aspects of the first handgun. Often we will be planning ahead and we should choose a handgun that will lead us to the ultimate goal, whether that goal is competition, hunting, or personal defense. You will be reasonably engaged in each pursuit with a good-quality handgun. If you wish to become a good all-around handgun shot, the .22 is an essential part of your battery. If you are not willing to practice more than absolutely necessary, then you may wish to work with a good center fire from the get go.

The middle of the road approach, I think, is ideal. Do not choose a handgun that is too small or too large or too weak or too powerful. Choose a common caliber. Take a look at reality and the chances are you will be able to proceed smoothly with the first handgun.

The Ruger .22/.45 features excellent human engineering. The controls are well placed for rapid and comfortable manipulation.

PART III

Recreational Handgun Training

CHAPTER 11

Just Making Brass

I HAVE A FRIEND WHO IS a firearms instructor. He claims he never goes to the range without a purpose. He always has a drill in mind to sharpen his skills or some new technique to try. I am certain he is a work in progress and good at what he does. I am equally certain that all work and no play makes for a dull boy.

I have been at this game a long time. Teaching personal defense is serious, but if there were not a flip side to the coin I probably would not be in the game for long. Recreational shooting with the handgun is a great sport. I have heard instructors tell their students that when they shoot and do not learn anything they are simply "making brass." I borrowed their term to describe fun shooting. Just making brass is a ball of fun that builds camaraderie, and while the hard-nosed drill sergeant types may disagree, making brass also builds skill.

The fun part of shooting may involve any type of handgun. But often enough we use a particular type of handgun whose primary function is recreational. This handgun does not have to defend my life, nor does it have to win a pistol match. It is not capable of dispatching a deer-sized animal. There is another name for making brass. It is called plinking. I am not sure where the term "plinking"

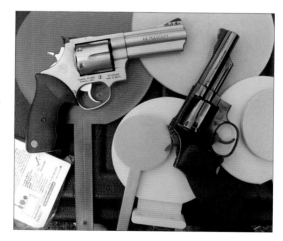

These are the bright and happy-looking Newbold targets. They absorb untold rounds of lead without complaint. At various ranges they have proven useful for training with both the .44 Magnum, top, and the .357 Magnum, bottom.

Our friend Lee Berry likes to fire at the postal contests offered by several periodicals. I bet he is the only shooter to perforate his target with a .30-caliber Mauser!

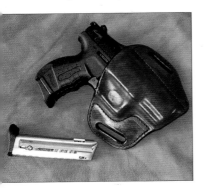

Just because you own a plinking-grade .22 doesn't mean you cannot obtain fine leather. This GDS holster is supplied for the Walther P22. This is good kit.

originated. Common wisdom holds that the sound of a .22-caliber bullet striking a tin can makes a resounding PLINK. I agree.

There are three main reasons we enjoy making brass so much. First, the pursuit is inexpensive. You may shoot all day for a pittance. A brick of 500 rounds of .22-caliber Winchester Wildcat ammunition is not out of the reach of anyone, and trust me, after the first 300 rounds even the most enthusiastic shooter is nearing his or her limit. Both expense and effort are minimal. Even when you elect to post up an informal paper target you are not striving for match-grade accuracy. You are just making brass. The second reason for enjoying plinking is freedom of choice. You have no time limit, but set your own pace. I have always held that firing at targets at known and unknown ranges is a better test of the shooter's ability than firing at a paper target at a known range. You may learn more about what the handgun and the shooter are capable of achieving, but be careful! You are only making brass not learning marksmanship, at least, according to the experts. A bottom line, however, must always be observed. There is nothing in the making brass or plinking game that allows the shooter in any way, shape, or form to violate safety rules. Be certain of a back stop and to always follow standard safety rules.

I love to shoot, and my job title includes a post at a law enforcement magazine with a column called Munitions. At the *Journal, Voice of American Law Enforcement* (the Journalonline.net) I sit down with the latest handgun, fire it carefully off the bench rest, and be certain that the piece is reliable and accurate enough for the job. It isn't always easy, and my results must be repeatable and verifiable. After all of that mental and physical effort, I need sublimation. I take the latest Glock 10mm or Smith & Wesson Military and Police (M&P) handgun in hand and do some fun shooting! I end up learning a lot about the handgun. I repeat: I never allow the urge to plink to overcome safety habits. I do, however, occasionally engage in hip shooting and instinctive fire just to see if there

The little Taurus .22 features a heavy barrel, adjustable sights, rubberized grips, and a decent enough trigger action. Light and pocketable, the .22 is a fine trail gun and plinker.

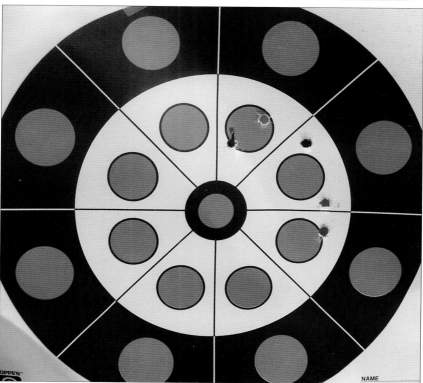

This is the Uncle Mike's Dartboard target. While this shooter didn't exactly ace the bull's-eye, the object is to plant bullets like darts.

is anything to it. There isn't anything of practical value there, but the occasionally brilliant shot is pure fun and exhilarating.

In plinking there is a great difference. In competition, you need a lot of good hits to iron out the occasional miss and still maintain a respectable final score. Much the same is true of personal-defense qualification. In plinking you can miss all day and the occasional brilliant hit, such as hitting a tin can at one hundred yards with a .38 Super- makes it all worthwhile. You may also try load combinations of little value elsewhere. As an example, stuffing a spoonful of fast-burning powder in the .38 Super case and topping the case with a 90-grain XTP yields some 1,600 feet per second. This is heady stuff, and the bullet flies straight enough to do some meaningful plinking to about 125 yards. Prairie dogs and coyote are well advised to stay under cover in this type of threat.

The sheer volume of .22-caliber ammunition fired in plinking every year makes all other calibers pale in comparison as a plinker, but just the same, there is no better fun than firing a big-bore handgun at ridiculous range. I have fired the Colt Single Action .45 at one hundred yards to confirm the words of Elmer Keith. He noted that the old horse soldiers relied upon the Colt because it was accurate enough to hit an Indian war pony at one hundred yards. My examples are 4 3/4-inch and 5 1/2-inch barrel revolvers not the longer barrel 7 1/2-inch cavalry guns, but just the same my results were encouraging. There was a lot of experimentation with bullet alloys not quite as hard as most of the store

Young Mr. Holt is learning to shoot with the Ruger Hunter, a special version of the Ruger .22 with a fluted barrel and fiber optic front sight. This is a good trainer and fine all-around rimfire pistol.

Make shooting a family affair. This family is enjoying a range outing under the watchful eye of an NRA-certified instructor.

bore alloys. The present companies seem to have settled on the old Lawrence cast-bullet formula, which works fine for most uses, but by casting a little soft and dropping a heavier bullet from the mold, I came up with a first-class bullet that delivered awfully good accuracy.

What did I accomplish? The war pony or the warrior would be out of luck with a sharp-eyed trooper lining up on him from one hundred yards. I confirmed that fact and had a fine time doing so.

The 10mm and the .38 Super automatics are great fun at long range as well. The .357 Magnum Smith & Wesson revolver is so accurate it is almost cheating to use a good solid Model 27. I load the Tennessee Valley bullets 190-grain flat point over Winchester 231 in .38 Special cases as a long-range load in the .357 Magnum. Micro Click adjustable sights and a superbly made handgun on humble tin cans at one hundred yards isn't much of a match. Here is a tip: .38 Special brass, heavy hard-cast bullets, Winchester 231 powder. Lots of practice. All of a sudden that fifty-yard deer doesn't seem quite so difficult—but we are only making brass!

At shorter range there are quite a few household items that are useful. (Never, never use glass or litter the range!) That rotten melon or tomatoes that have been in the fridge a tad too long are great targets. Be certain you leave them in a spot that is biodegradable or where the crows will find them. Those little animal crackers also make excellent silhouette targets for practice for the real thing. I am not certain shooting steel gongs qualifies as just making brass because we use them in competition pretty often. But gongs are great fun.

This shooter is wringing out a Walther P38 on the range. Old guns such as this 1943 9mm are a ball of fun on the range and give good historical insight.

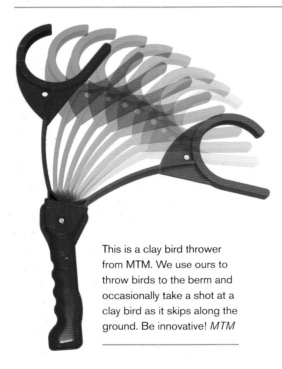

This is a clay bird thrower from MTM. We use ours to throw birds to the berm and occasionally take a shot at a clay bird as it skips along the ground. Be innovative! *MTM*

At my favorite range they are well set up, directing bullets into the ground at the base of the target as good steel reaction targets should. Gongs tell quite a story for those with an ear for accuracy. If you strike the gong in the center, it will move to the rear. If you strike to the left or right of dead center, it spins to one side or the other. Too high or too low and it does not give the satisfying straight to the rear movement that we all strive for. Gongs give instant feedback without the need to walk to the target and set the paper up time and again.

I enjoy steel gong targets very much. I also enjoy firing at Mike Gibson's steel targets. MGM (Mike Gibson Manufacturing) produces some of the most appropriate and useful steel targets of all time. When struck, the targets are pushed to the rear against spring pressure. The spring back and you hammer them again. A good shot with a heavy handgun may keep the steel moving.

As for myself there is nothing more enjoyable than the MGM popper, a good 1911, and a cast bullet hand-load using the Oregon Trail 180-grain SWC at about 850 feet per second. There is a version of the Gibson Pepper Popper for the .22-caliber handgun I find especially appropriate for making brass. These targets are durable and affordable and offer perhaps the best learning experience in plinking.

I have also used NewBold self-sealing nonsplatter target with excellent results. The NewBold targets are synthetic and react when hit but do not produce the gong sound. These targets register hits, but they will take hundreds perhaps thousands of hits without any sign of damage. There is no splatter. The sound is different from steel targets, but they are a great resource and get the job done. Dueling trees and the like are also excellent resources for the great unproclaimed sport of handgun plinking.

At this point you may ask what the best handgun is for pure recreational shooting. Anything will make brass, but there are better choices than others. I think that perhaps the all-time great fun gun of the century is the Ruger Standard Model .22. Inexpensive, easily learned, reliable, and accurate, the Standard Model has much to recommend. The standard model is a great pistol for use with one of my favorite tricks. I set two tin cans on top of the other. I impress my friends with my ability to perforate both and send each spinning. I take a careful aim at the lower can and fire twice as quickly as possible. The first can is hit and goes sailing, the second can falls and is struck. My friends think I am a great trick shot, but the real trick is to focus on the lower can, take a perfect sight picture, and fire a double tap as quickly as possible. You will get both cans. You cannot do that with a revolver, and the Standard Model builds skills rather quickly; but keep the trick between us to preserve my reputation.

If like many of us you appreciate the romance and thrill of the Old West then you probably need a single-action revolver. The Ruger Single Six revolver is ideal for those lazy evenings when you are reliving *High Plains Drifter* and facing the humble tin can with a single-action hog leg in hand. You will learn to appreciate sight picture and sight alignment and realize that the shot being fired at the moment is the important shot. There isn't much opportunity for a fast follow-up shot with the single-action. The Ruger is far more rugged than any other single-action revolver and will afford you many hours of fun and peace of mind.

One of the greatest plinkers of all time is getting difficult to find, but if you are able to locate one at a fair price, snatch it up. This is the High Standard Double Nine. The Double Nine is a double-action revolver with swing-out cylinder, but it looks like a single-action revolver. The Double Nine is a first-class all-around plinker that offers the best of both worlds. They may be cocked for single-action shooting, but they are not as ponderously slow to load as the single-action. There are other handguns available only through the used market that take a bit of hunting, but they are worth the wait.

The Colt New Frontier Single Action .22 is a downsized Colt Single Action Army with many good features. There is something classy about this handgun,

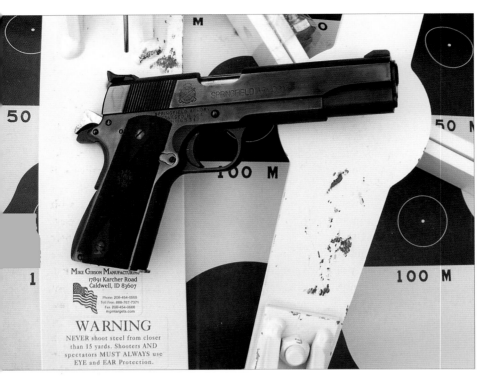

Take a good .45 such as this middle-of-the-road Springfield, a Gibson Pepper Popper, plenty of ammunition, and you have the makings of a fine day at making brass.

and I have never met one that was not accurate. Avoid the aluminum-frame Colt .22 handguns as balance and longevity are not as good. Another good revolver that is difficult to find is the Colt Official Police in .22 caliber. This is another handgun well worth the search. Smith & Wesson double-action .22-caliber revolvers are awfully pricey of late, but then they are well made of good material and remain the premium double-action revolver. Among the all-time favorite pistols for informal practice is the Colt Woodsman .22 automatic. Slim, graceful, and accurate this is a first-class automatic handgun.

There are light .22-caliber handguns that are particularly useful for impressing your friends. The Beretta Model 21A, as an example, is far more accurate than anyone would have a right to believe. It is useful for plinking to some twenty-five yards. The Walther PPK .22 is another neat little pistol, but in my experience it is not as reliable as the more modern Walther P22. The Bersa .22 seems to be among the more reliable and accurate small-frame .22-caliber handguns. They are not as accurate as the Ruger Standard Model pistols, but they are pocketable and useful. Always remember, when plinking there is no real reason to carry the handgun holstered with the chamber loaded. I would recommend always keeping the .22

chamber empty, particularly the versions with a concealed hammer or striker fired mechanism.

You are by no means limited to making brass only with the .22. Among my favorite plinking handguns are double-action .38 police revolvers and the .45 automatic. I recently loaded five hundred rounds of .38 Special in new Starline brass expressly for plinking. I used inexpensive cast bullets from Rim Rock bullets, one of my favorite suppliers. This time I used a modest charge of TiteGroup powder for about 750 feet per second. Firing the Colt Official Police revolver double-action and going for speed-developed double-action revolver skills rather quickly. The 1911 .45 is a blast. You need light loads and the majority of 1911 handguns will function with 180-grain bullets at about 800 feet per second.

At the time of this writing, I had just finished off a batch of 500 .45s loaded with the Oregon Trail 180-grain SWC bullets, among the most accurate bullets ever cast. This is simply a great training aid and I am never embarrassed for firing lighter than standard loads and just having a ball. The high-capacity 9mm handguns are also great fun. When you have fourteen to seventeen rounds on tap, there is a tendency to have fun mowing down a row of tin cans or keeping a reaction target going. I am glad to have a good supply of the Oregon Trail 124-grain hard-cast bullets on hand for the 9mm.

When you choose a plinking handgun give some consideration to the other members of your family. The spouse and children may one day take up your hobby, and a handgun that is consistent with their hand size and level of interest is a good choice. You could do a lot worse than managing to interest the family in the fine sport of Making Brass.

You can never have enough ammunition close at hand! This MTM Caseguard belt carrier makes digging for .22s far more accessible. *MTM*

CHAPTER 12

Competition Shooting

JUST ABOUT EVERYONE LIKES COMPETITIVE sports. Some like fishing and some like golf. When competition is at its best you are competing against yourself, striving for your personal best. Stress is external, but determination is internal. As an example, in personal-defense shooting the motivation is external. You wish to survive. But in the shooting games, the motivation to excel becomes internal.

COMPETITION SHOOTING: BULL'S-EYE

I have to admit that IDPA and IPSC matches are pretty darned exciting. These matches seem to capture the hearts and minds of young shooters in particular. But in sheer numbers and investment, the handgun sport known as bull's-eye is still at the top of the list. Bull's-eye shooting is demanding of both the shooter and the equipment used, and this appeals to many people. Bull's-eye shooting appears simple at first, but the physical and mental disciplines involved are more complex that many realize.

THE GAME

The 2700 is the standard pistol match fired in bull's-eye. You fire a total of 270 shots. The value of each shot is a maximum of ten points. I have always been fascinated by the fact that the game demands the use of three pistols: a .22, a center-fire .38 or 9mm, and the .45. Each pistol is fired to the tune of 90 rounds.

Shooting a bull's-eye competition is never easy. With time and skill you will be competitive. The author often practices with reduced-range rifle targets to master the handgun.

In the origins of the match the three-gun selection made perfect sense. The civilians used .22s, the cops used .38s, and the Army used .45s, but in bull's-eye each had to have a taste of t he other's discipline to compete. Everyone shot .22s and you also had to fire one or more of the big bores to be competitive. In the early days shooters used various .22-caliber pistols that were far less highly developed than those we see in use today. Peace officers used some of the finest revolvers ever made, including the Colt Officers Model Match and the Smith & Wesson K 38. Colt developed the National Match and the Gold Cup .45-caliber automatic pistols for bull's-eye shooters. Over time many shooters elected to shoot the .45 in the center-fire match. The .38 revolver died out in bull's-eye.

It is rare to see a fine Smith & Wesson Model 52 .38 Special self-loader competing today, and I would be surprised to see a revolver. Basically, the courses are now shot with the .22 and .45. At one time the .38s were considerably more accurate than the .45 and could make for a higher aggregate or total score. Today this is no longer true as there are many fine custom pistolsmiths turning out excellent bull's-eye guns. There are four matches in each 900-point shooting session. These include four disciplines: slow fire, the National Match Course, timed fire, and rapid fire. The match takes a while to study and learn, but we can give you a basic guide.

The slow-fire, timed-fire, and rapid-fire match courses are twenty-shot matches. The National Match course runs to thirty shots, ten shots slow fire at fifty yards, ten

Reaching the top tier of competition requires dedication and practice. This young man has more than a little talent at the game. *SIGARMS*

Cowboy action shooting is a special event well worth attending. These shooters are packing the usual two revolvers in special Western holsters.

shots each in timed, and rapid fire at twenty-five yards. Timed fire is five rounds in twenty seconds. Rapid fire is five shots in ten seconds. The neat thing about timed firing stages is that the targets are facing away from the shooter at the beginning of the match. The targets turn toward the shooter and then turn away again after the shots are fired or the time limit is over.

There are many variations on the theme. As an example, there are indoor ranges and other areas in which it is not possible to fire all match requirements at fifty yards. Reduced size targets are used. By the way, the X ring of the fifty-yard target measures about 1.7 inches in the X rings, and the bull or ten ring is 3.36 inches or so in diameter. Time limits are not onerous and fair to all concerned. A high score on the 2,700-point scale is the mark of an accomplished shooter. Everyone has a different idea of the toughness of the matches. Some excel in slow fire and simply cannot speed up; others do better in rapid fire. I have been told that sometimes the slow-fire shooter agonizes over the sight picture, takes too long to aim, realizes he is out of time, and then gets in a hurry and jerks the trigger. This mirrors my own experience during training classes.

This type of competition is good training for focus on sight picture, sight alignment, and follow through. As in most shooting disciplines, trigger compression is absolutely vital to successful bull's-eye work. Physical conditioning is also important. No matter how strong you may become there is some movement when

the handgun is held. The trick is to press the trigger when the sights are aligned properly. Practice is essential. Top competitors tell me that they may fire only once a week, but they dry fire three to four times a week, sometimes every day. A good safe dry fire regimen is essential to keeping the edge.

The shooting stance cannot be overemphasized. A solid, repeatable shooting stance and proper feet position leads to good accuracy. You need to learn a natural point that is

Homegrown matches might include "dueling trees." These targets emphasize quick reaction and target feedback.

comfortable and ends with the handgun at eye level pointed toward the target. The excitement of the game is felt in your heart when the command to load is heard, followed by ready on the right, then ready on the firing line, and finally the command to fire. The game demands absolute concentration. You cannot worry about what the man or woman beside you is doing or what their score is or even noises in the crowd. You need to be in your own little world. All that is important is the sights and the target.

The beginner sometimes tries to get by on the cheap, but you really need good equipment from the get go. You will penalize yourself and proficiency will come at a snail's pace if you limit yourself with poor equipment. Remember, you are in a game that demands the handgun be capable of three-inch groups at fifty yards. It may be a good long haul before you are able to fire a group measuring twice that size at fifty yards, but the handgun should be capable of that type of accuracy. There are good gunsmiths turning out quality bull's-eye guns. Rock River Arms once offered factory pistols of the bull's-eye type. Currently, Les Baer pistols and the Colt Gold Cup might be the front runners in the center fire matches. In .22 caliber, the Smith & Wesson Model 41 is practically the only choice among top competitors, or otherwise, a highly modified Ruger .22. Look to Power Custom and Volquartsen for custom .22-caliber versions of the Ruger Standard Model.

INTERNATIONAL DEFENSE PISTOL ASSOCIATION

International Defense Pistol Association (IDPA) matches were founded to give shooters a level playing field and to test their skills in reality-based exercises. The main goal of IDPA is to test the skill and ability of the individual, not the equipment. (This is a paraphrase from the IDPA rulebook that I feel sums up the game.) As for the guns used, there are several classes of firearms used and all compete in a fair test. The IDPA rulebook does not approve or disapprove of any one type of handgun but rather approves several handgun classes, such as single-action or double-action autoloaders and revolver classes, and the shooter competes in the class with other like-minded shooters. Only handguns of 9mm or larger, in the case of self-loaders, or the .38 revolver or larger are approved. The handguns that are used are the same type that are in use every day for concealed carry and personal protection. Long slide automatics or pistols with optical sights are not permitted. It is generally encouraged that competitors use stock guns; however, quite a number of us use custom handguns as a matter or course for concealed carry.

I would not wish to be prohibited from using my Action Works .45 simply because I wanted the best in a carry gun. There are allowances for custom sights and aftermarket parts such as barrels. But the pistols are stock in appearance. Custom grips and Bar Sto barrels are common. The pistol may be custom, but the bottom line is that the pistol is a practical personal-defense handgun. As an example, among the most popular handguns used in IDPA is the Beretta 92. The Beretta is reliable, it is the Army gun, and 9mm ammunition such as Winchester

This shooter is practicing firing from cover. IDPA and IPSC both stress firing from cover during some stages.

Firing from a kneeling position requires discipline. Note the .40-caliber Beretta kicks much more from this position.

This is all you need to compete in IDPA: a good factory handgun like the Beretta Cougar and a good supply of reliable ammunition and you're good to go.

white box is plentiful. While less expensive handguns are often used, the Beretta is a good choice.

All of the draws in IDPA are from concealed carry, usually the typical concealed carry or photographers vest. Holsters are a varied lot and none of the special competition rigs are allowed. What is allowed is the type of holster that many of us carry for personal defense. These include strong side holsters, inside the waistband holsters, and practical holsters that are usable in the real world. Several makers produce a special version of the strong side holster for IDPA use. Among these is the Haugen Handgun Leather holster called appropriately the IDPA. A good strong side holster such as this is a fine starting point. I have also used a quality strong side Avenger-style holster from Ward Leather with good results.

In my experience, shooters joining the IDPA usually own the pistol then look into the rulebook to determine which class to compete in. With IDPA so large these days and new shooters coming on board, some will study the rulebook and then decide which handgun to purchase. IDPA shooters are a friendly bunch and will be glad to welcome you on board. My recommendation for a first-time handgun for IDPA shooting is either a good-quality four-inch barrel revolver in .38 Special or .357 Magnum caliber or a good-quality double-action 9mm pistol. You cannot go wrong with the Beretta M 9 or Beretta 92, and the SIG is never a bad choice. Stock up on reliable ammunition. Some of us at the gun club recently obtained Seller and Bellot 9mm by the caseload and have enjoyed good service.

When shooting IDPA, there is no place for optical sights, muzzle brakes, or compensators. While compensators are used in the open class in some other shooting disciplines, they have no place in match competition that mirrors self-defense training. A compensator held below eye level might throw lead, powder, or pieces of the bullet jacket into the eyes of the shooter. No muzzle brake compensator or suppressor may be used in IDPA competition. IDPA founders had several reasons for limiting the types of handguns you could use. First, the rules reinforce shooter skill foremost. The IDPA match would not become an equipment race. The shooter with the best sponsor or the most bucks would not win the match. There would be a level playing field.

The rules are intended to encourage shooters to shoot the handgun that they carry on the street. There should not be a carry gun and an IDPA gun. Finally, the IDPA box was designed to gauge the size of competing pistols. The IDPA gun box has inside dimensions of 8 3/4 inches x 6 inches x 1 5/8 inches.

Revolvers are exempt, but there are rules concerning revolvers. (My Springfield Long Slide 1911 will not fit this box and neither will my Les Baer Monolith. Nothing for me to cry about.)

These shooters are discussing the next course of fire. Chances are they will come up with something that will challenge the competitors.

Here are the IDPA categories:

Service pistol matches: If your pistol is a 9mm and does not weigh more than thirty-nine ounces you are good to go for service pistol matches.

Enhanced service pistol: These matches are limited to pistols of 9mm or larger, with a maximum weight of forty-three ounces.

Custom defensive pistol: Self-loaders of .45 caliber with a gross unloaded weight of no more than forty-two ounces compete in this one, as long as they meet the box test.

Enhanced service revolver: These revolvers must chamber a caliber of 9mm or greater and may use moon clips to compete. Barrel length is limited to a little more than four inches. But some of these revolvers weigh fifty ounces, a healthy chunk of steel! Revolvers with eight-round capacity are limited to six shots on tap in this class.

Stock service revolver: These are the .38-caliber or larger revolvers, and moon clips are not allowed.

The rules in IDPA tend to encourage service-grade handguns. As such this is the game most appropriate for personal-defense shooters; however, I know many shooters who enjoy IDPA yet they do not carry a concealed handgun as a matter of course. IDPA is enjoyable and does not require a great cash outlay. You probably already own a pistol suitable for IDPA use. The IDPA is ideal for those who want

Erik Lund, a well known shooter sponsored by SIG, is well prepared for the match ahead. *SIGARMS*

to keep their shooting skills sharp for personal defense.

INTERNATIONAL PRACTICAL SHOOTING COMPETITION

The International Practical Shooting Competition (IPSC) is among the first highly organized shooting sports intended to promote personal-defense skills. IPSC engages many shooters who are not police or military. The majority are simply citizens who enjoy action shooting. The origins of IPSC go back to the 1950s Leather Slap at Big Bear Lake, California, where Colonel Jeff Cooper and other like-minded shooters competed against one another. The sport grew by leaps and bounds, and eventually there was a need for greater structure and for rules, dues, and larger facilities. The International Pistol Conferences held in Columbia, Missouri, in 1976 was the founding moment for modern IPSC. The

Many top shooters shoot three gun matches with the shotgun, rifle, and handgun. This triples the challenge. *SIGARMS*

basic elements that are important to IPSC shooting are accuracy power and speed. This is often expressed in the Latin terms *diligentia, vis, celeritas*: accuracy, power, and speed.

These elements are important in all forms of shooting, and in IPSC they are kept in balance. The targets used are representations of the human form, similar to the standard FBI silhouette that has been taken to represent a five-foot ten-inch 190-pound man. There are five divisions, allowing shooters of every type and stripe to participate, from beginner to experienced shooter. It is interesting that the sport that began purely as a practical shooting exercise has evolved into a true sport. Karate and fencing have similar origins and have emerged as exciting legitimate sports. IPSC is among the most exciting of the shooting sports, with disciplines involving multiple targets, moving targets, and small targets at longer ranges. There are targets that react when hit, and there is stress on competitive strategies. The IPSC requires a more advanced target handgun than the IDPA. Many shooters enjoy their personal custom handguns used in these matches very much.

METALLIC SILHOUETTE

Along with the poinsettia, there are a number of good things to come from Mexico. Salma Hayek comes to mind. Next, my good friends Luis and Antonio. Then, long-range silhouette shooting.

Fast draw is a great test of men and leather gear. These competitors from a few years ago paved the way for modern fast-draw shooters. Bob Munden is among the best known fast-draw shooters. *Bob Munden*

Legend has it that Pancho Villa and his men sharpened their skills at long range with silhouette shooting, even sometimes using live animals. By 1950 the sport involved metal silhouettes in the form of animals. In the 1970s the sport came to Arizona and became popular quickly. The International Handgun Metallic Silhouette Association was founded in 1976. Metal chickens, turkeys, pigs, and rams are addressed with handgun fire at long range. There are various stages to overcome beginning at ten meters and running to one hundred meters. I have looked over the sights of an 8 3/8-inch barrel Smith & Wesson at the longer range and that chicken looks mighty small. I have also engaged in falling chicken matches, using reduced steel plates at shorter range, and the game remains challenging. Given sufficient land the ranges often extend further.

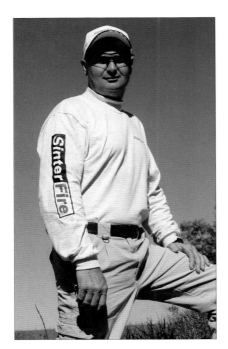

Competition pistol shooting is a big business. Todd Jarrett is sponsored by Sinterfire bullets. These sponsors keep the shooting sports alive. *SinterFire*

The smallest target, the chicken, may be placed at fifty yards and the largest, the ram, at two hundred yards. It is interesting to note that if you hit the target but only rock the target and not bring it down, this hit is counted as a miss. The target must go down, just as you would expect a game animal to go down with one well placed shot. The time for each shot, two minutes, is generous, but the skill involved is considerable. Anyone wishing to compete will be able to without highly specialized equipment. As an example, the .22-caliber category is lively. The production category is limited to factory stock handguns, including single-shot pistols.

The revolver matches are shot with some of the most accurate and powerful revolvers ever made. Some are large, heavy, and specialized, but of late, the production .500 dwarfs what we once regarded as an oversize handgun. When getting started, finding the match and showing up is the first step. I have seen shooters show up with old High Standard Double Nine .22-caliber revolvers. While they were not competitive, they were off to a good start. I shot an 8 3/8-inch Smith & Wesson K 22 for several years in the .22-caliber matches. A Ruger Super Blackhawk in .44 Magnum is an affordable beginning. I have used the Oregon Trail 240-grain SWC with excellent results at long range in .44 Magnum caliber. The majority of the matches will be fifty meters contests, and the two hundred meter ranges are not that easy to find. But persevere and you will find that range and find your spot in the scheme of things.

PPC

The Practical Police game is popular and is shot in courses similar to the average police qualification. With a few basic adaptations, the PPC course is what we used to quality in the "old days" at the PD. The PPC course is divided into four segments at seven, twenty-five, and fifty yards. The course of fire is as follows:

Sixty Rounds

Stage one: 12 rounds in 20 seconds at 21 feet
Stage two: 18 rounds in 90 seconds at 75 feet
Stage three: 6 rounds in 12 seconds at 75 feet
Stage four: 24 rounds in 165 seconds at feet

If you are using a revolver, all the shots must be fired double-action except for the shots fired at fifty yards. PPC is an interesting discipline that many working cops find is good training. PPC is demanding and requires great user skill to be in the top tiers, but remember we started somewhere.

FAST DRAW

Fast draw is a true shooting sport but one that is most often fired with blanks. The firearms used are special single-action revolvers that are heavily modified with aluminum barrels for light weight. The shooters stands in the fast-draw stance and draws and fires in a fraction of a second.

The blank cartridge either activates a timer or bursts a balloon. Fast draw is a challenge to the human brain and concentration. When you see a video of someone like the great Bob Munden drawing, you wonder if he feels match pressure or match nerves. He moves so fast you cannot follow with the eye. He has certainly mastered the minimum arc of movement. Fast draw is highly specialized. With the greater interest in cowboy action shooting, it is interesting to note that fast draw remains quite popular. A true challenge, fast draw is a wonderful sport both for the participant and the spectator.

CHAPTER 13

Hunting

HANDGUN HUNTING IS THE MOST demanding firearm discipline. Bow hunting may be as challenging, but then it is not a firearms sport. The bottom line is this: Handgun hunting is difficult on every level. The stalk, getting into position for the shot, working your way within range, and making the shot are difficult.

There are handguns that resemble rifles, with their sixteen-inch barrels and optical sights. They are credible hunting firearms, but they do not fit into my worldview. I stick with a powerful revolver and a cartridge beginning with four. To each his own. The X-frame Smith & Wesson revolvers are the newest rendition of Smith & Wesson's Magnum revolver. The .460 Smith & Wesson is a world-class hunter with a flat trajectory and great accuracy. The .500 Smith & Wesson Magnum has unprecedented smash. Either is a good example of the gunmaker's art, with long-range capabilities unheard of in a revolver. The bar has been raised considerably by these handguns.

With proper optical sights, as one example, the .460 Smith & Wesson is easily a two hundred-yard game getter. I understand the hunter who hunts with the Contender single-shot pistol well. He does so for the challenge, and he is a shooter to be respected. Often, when hunting with a rifle, I use a Taylor and Company 1874 Sharps. I love the single-shot rifle and enjoy it as a pure hunting tool. Perhaps I am not up to the challenge of a single-shot pistol, but all of us must remember that chances are we will have only one shot at game. As such, a fast follow-up shot may not be necessary, but when hunting large game at close range, the powerful .44 Magnum is a great comfort.

The Smith & Wesson Model 25 in .45 Colt is a sure killer at moderate range. The author prefers this handgun to the .44 Magnum inside of fifty yards.

My personal hunting handguns reflect the philosophy of Elmer Keith. A good modern big-bore revolver is a firearm of opportunity. The handgun rides easily on the hip in a Cannon Leather holster, as long as the handgun does not go over fifty ounces. A Smith & Wesson , Taurus, or Ruger Magnum is accurate enough for the intended task as long as it has good sights and adequate power and we have practiced. The sights and trigger action are important. The front sight should be a bold ramp, and the rear sight should be fully adjustable if our quarry is to be approached at ranges of thirty-five yards or more.

General-purpose handguns are often best served with moderate length barrels. Dedicated handgun hunters need a longer barrel of 6-inch, 7 1/2-inch, or even 8 3/8-inch length. A Ruger Super Blackhawk with 7 1/2-inch barrel is capable of taking game to one hundred yards or more. But short-range hunting is more common. Among my fondest memories is standing over a large boar hog with the steam rising from .44 Magnum bullet hole. The range was short and gunhandling is as important as marksmanship. But that is the aftermath.

Among the author's favorite revolvers are the Taurus Tracker handguns. The Tracker has created a new baseline and a new standard for comparison. *Taurus*

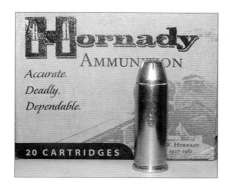

The Hornady Custom loads in .44 Magnum are among the most versatile and accurate of all Magnum loads. The XTP bullet is still a fascinating projectile years after its smashing introduction.

You have to practice hard to become a competent hunter. This Newbold target represents the kill zone of a thin-skinned animal. The range at which all of your shots are in this target area is the kill zone.

Two choices: For short range, the 4-inch barrel Colt Anaconda .44 Magnum is a good choice. The 8 3/8-inch barrel model 629 develops greater velocity and accuracy.

The proper choice of handgun, caliber, and ammunition is one step. Many hours of practice and range time are important to mastering the big bores. You must know the handgun and your own capabilities inside and out. Respect for the animal demands no less. Some hunters begin with a handgun and proceed to master the sport but use a rifle when the range is predictably long. Others hunt primarily with a rifle but use a handgun on occasion. Others become fascinated with the challenge of handgun hunting and seldom hunt with anything other than a handgun.

The first and most logical question is what type of game are you hunting? Next, at what range is the game encountered? It isn't logical to attempt some type of hunts with the typical packing handgun with a four- or five-inch barrel. Standard calibers may not be well suited to heavy skinned game. One of my good friends took two separate hunts with a rifle. These hunts made him into a handgun hunter. In the first

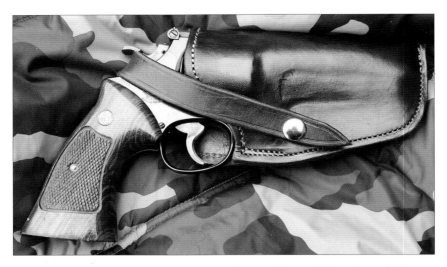

This is a classic hunter for brush country. The Smith & Wesson N frame is carried in a Lobo Leather Threepersons holster.

hunt he took a big Russian Boar with a .44 Magnum carbine at about fifteen yards. The only thing he could see in the four-power scope mounted on his Marlin was bristle and tusks! During a second hunt he took a black bear with a .30-06 rifle at a short twenty paces. Either animal could have been taken with the .44 Magnum revolver. Power is one defining factor and for most of us this means the factory-loaded .41 Magnum, the .44 Magnum, or the .454 Casull. The .45 Colt with handloads may be added to this list.

Remember, only modern super-strong .45 Colts such as the Ruger Super Blackhawk are suitable for use with heavy hunting loads. For light-skinned game such as deer the .357 Magnum will do the business at moderate range,

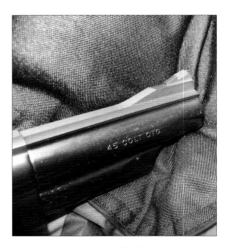

When you are using a Smith & Wesson, the classic ramp front sight and orange sight insert are a great aid in marksmanship. Insist on the best.

but many of us consider the .357 Magnum light for hunting anything other than medium-size deer. Range and power dictate the game. Due to the loss of energy and drop of standard calibers, Magnum cartridges are better suited for use past fifty yards, with all due respect to the .44 Special and .45 Auto Rim.

The Smith & Wesson .45 Colt caliber revolver is a great field gun. The cylinder isn't as thick as the .44 Magnum, so respect pressure limitations when handloading.

Many pursuits are well suited to the handgun hunter. Boar Hunting is a head-long pursuit that often ends with a shot at short range. At shorter ranges, the standard calibers work just fine. The heavy-loaded .44 Special has about the same energy at five yards as the .44 Magnum does at one hundred yards, as an example. A hard cast SWC bullet will shoot through a wild hog or a deer. The .44 Magnum and the .454 Casull are more powerful and more accurate at longer range than the standard calibers.

It is important that each hunter begin with a handgun of a good size and weight, with a recoil-dampening long barrel and suitably comfortable grips. The Magnums kick like a mule and are not suitable for the newly christened handgun hunter of little handgun experience. Of course, they can be mastered and no they will not break bones, but you must respect the power and momentum of these handguns. Just the same, the often given advice of beginning with a .357 Magnum revolver may not be the best advice. Rather than beginning with a heavy-frame .357 and working up to a .44, you may just as easily begin with the big bore and work up the totem pole in load power. But then you have to be a handloader.

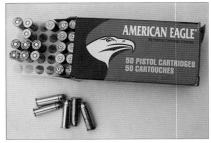

Buffalo Bore ammunition maximizes handguns' calibers for hunting. This 170-grain JHP in .44 Special breaks 1,150 feet per second. With real accuracy this is a fine deer load at moderate range.

Even off the shelf, .44 Magnum loads have plenty of killing power and accuracy. The American Eagle load is high quality and plenty strong.

With handloads, most of the .44's diet may be inexpensive loads that mimic the .44 Special and then you may approach different power levels as you advance in proficiency. That said, most of us have learned the nuances of handloading with the .357 Magnum, and it is a fine long-range cartridge as far as accuracy goes. With proper handloads, the .357 Magnum is well suited to thin-skinned game and the big cats at moderate range and for pests at long range.

When I hunt with a handgun, I realize that hunting is what you make of it. For many of us, the nervous exhilaration of utter solitude is the most important component of hunting. Finding a wild place to open your soul is worthwhile. I treasure my memories of hunting in the bare willows and cottonwoods. The exquisite solitude of a winter morning and fox tracks in the snow are difficult to explain to those who have not been there. I suppose I am one of those with a demented appreciation for an arduous and soggy trek.

When hunting, any game animal is respected. I will respect a squirrel with a .22 and use the adequate .44 Magnum for boar hogs. The importance of a good .22 for practice has been stated, and the .22 is also a good hunter. If you are able to stalk closely enough, the .44 Magnum is enough for hunting most animals. When hunting with the handgun there is less meat damage and you may eat right up to the bullet hole without the excess of ruined meat seen with some rifle calibers.

Taking game is demanding of both men and firearms. It would take a volume to discuss the tactics needed for each animal. Calling predators such as coyote is great excitement, as they are very foxy. You will fire from a braced position in a solid blind. When hunting fox, there are lighter calibers that will do a good job. These include the heavy loaded .38 Special, 9mm Luger, and .38 ACP Super. Hunting deer from a high, elaborate tree stand is much the same but demands at least a .357 Magnum revolver. Whatever the game, you must test your skill and match the gun and this skill to the game.

If the shot is likely to occur at fifty yards then you need to be able to place all of your shots in the kill zone of the animal at that range. The man who is able to connect with a handgun against a deer-sized animal at a long one hundred yards and put the bullet into the boiler room is an uncommonly good shot, but he exists. This man may be shooting right up to the capabilities of the handgun. The scoped .454 is another matter, capable of good hits well past one hundred yards. My standards of comparison are the Ruger Super Blackhawk .44 Magnum and the long-barrel Smith & Wesson revolvers. There are more efficient hunters but none that I have mastered.

Before you begin in the field you must thoroughly research the game you are pursuing. Handgun hunting is a challenge with a goal beyond simply taking meat. It is a challenge to both men and firearms. While not ideal, a handful of sighting in shots are often adequate for the rifleman. Handgun hunters must go to greater lengths to be certain that their firearms are properly sighted for different ranges and that they understands the hold-over or drop at different ranges. A rifleman may simply study drop tables, the handgun hunter must shoot to confirm. The point of impact may differ between if you use wooden or rubber grips, and this must be explored and verified. A handgun hunter puts considerable effort into handgun marksmanship, gun handling, range estimation, and recoil control. Some take to handgun hunting like a duck to water; others have a difficult time of it but eventually succeed.

Competition is a means of gaining skill and experience. Thirty years ago I shot silhouette competition, firing at small steel representations of game animals including goat, deer, and turkey. Ranges were longer than common in the wild and the challenge was there. I used a Smith & Wesson double-action revolver but always fired single-action, just as almost everyone will do in the field. I won several matches and found my marksmanship skill improving with every match. These wins represented hard work. I often fired as many as five hundred rounds a week in practice. I was doing so to win the matches but also to build all-around skill, although the game itself became a thing with its own importance.

I was on the road to becoming a good all-around shooter. A fellow whose name I wish I recalled always gave me a run for the money. He was constantly in the top two or three shooters. I will never forget the look of concentration he had as he looked over the sights of his Super Blackhawk. Then one day this cool calm shooter won a match. He went on to dominate the course for weeks. He was primarily a hunter, and he worked the matches to stay sharp.

KILL ZONES

The kill zone of a deer is about eight inches. Your sure kill zone is the range at which you are able to keep all of your shots in an eight-inch circle. Your personal skills set the range, whether it is twenty-five, fifty, sixty, or seventy-five yards. Practical accuracy is the concern. A Colt Single Action Army or USFA Rodeo in .45 Colt is perfectly capable of taking a deer inside of thirty-five yards, within the limits of fixed sights. The combination of practical and intrinsic accuracy must be there. The power of the cartridge is a limiting factor. I have taken deer cleanly with the .45 ACP, but the range was short and each was an opportunity rather than a planned event. I have always felt that short-range power is the forte of the Magnum revolver. Today both technology and sighting equipment have given us a new baseline.

There is an able minority of handgunners who have grown to feel limited by the .44 Magnum. These able few have demanded and gotten more powerful handguns in the form of the .454 Casull and others. Rather than moving to a rifle when limited by the range and effect of the .44 Magnum, they have taken up the far more difficult task of mastering the .454 Casull. For those so inclined to try the .454 Casull, I have this advice. First, fry up a mess of bull gonads in the southern fashion with seasoned brown gravy. They are quite good, although an acquired taste—similar to chicken gizzards. A few meals like this and your nerve will be fortified enough to take on the mighty .454.

Seriously, the .454 is not for the sheepish, but it will do at 150 yards what the .44 Magnum will do at 100, roughly speaking. If you are hunting plains game and the size of the game and the range dictates a more powerful cartridge, then the .454 is a sure thing in trained hands. When you realize the game is out of reach, you need to do a few calculations. Range and the needed penetration in hide and bone are necessary parts of the equation. When you have this model down you may find that you are able to make hits past the effective range of the cartridge. Taking down a half ton of mass and muscle isn't easy. When the animal is dangerous, and all large animals may be dangerous at the right moment, there is no room for error.

This is the little giant. The author regards the .22 Magnum as one of the overall most useful of all handgun calibers.

Are you guaranteed a broad side shot? I may take a raking shot on a deer with a heavy loaded .45 Colt, with a 250-grain SWC at 1,050 feet per second at the muzzle, but the same shot would not be applicable to a Caribou. I use a rule of thumb. I calculate the range at which the .44 Magnum becomes a .44 Special. At long range, the Magnum becomes a .44 Russian. I am not hunting large game with a 750-feet per second .44 Russian. The .454 Casull has longer legs before it becomes just a .45 Colt. I am pretty certain I could make hits past the sure killing range of the .44 Magnum, and I respect these limitations.

There are means of testing both penetration and accuracy. Accuracy testing is straightforward on the range; simply use the likely position you will adopt in the field.

I use a stack of wet newsprint or old phonebooks suitably soaked overnight in a large tomato bucket to test hunting cartridges. A minimum of twenty-four inches of penetration in this media is needed for larger game. Decide what you are looking for, the size of the animal, and test your loading. If this penetration is maintained and you are making hits at a certain range, this is your killing range.

PESTS AND VARMINTS

When it comes to the big cats, fox, and coyote, a fast opening JHP is needed. Familiarity with the handgun and a bit of practice in fast handling goes a long way. When testing the load for this smaller game I like to use one of the Nosler JHP bullets. If the game is larger I use the Hornady XTP. Here's a tip: The chest shot is okay, but if you are able to take a raking shot that goes through the entire body then the effect on the game is often immediate. Mountain lions and cougars have been taken with light calibers, but I do not subscribe to this. The .357 Magnum is ideal.

There was an experienced explorer in the Amazon who took seven jaguars with the .357 Magnum. His documented successes impressed him. The .357 Magnum, he concluded, would do the work of a rifle but was much easier to carry. That says a lot about handgun hunting. I have wandered in the woods intermittently for some

Sometimes you have to have a rifle. Handgun hunters often match their rifles and pistols in the same caliber. This is a pair of .44 Magnum firearms.

forty years. I have deployed appropriate gear. Early on I went with what I could afford. I have interviewed many handgun hunters and attempted to be a witness rather than an onlooker. If there is a common thread among successful hunters it is skill building and respect for game animals. Proficiency is simple to acquire but not easy.

AIMING AND PRACTICE

Do you know where the heart and lungs are located in your quarry? I often ask hunters and I learn that some are mistaken concerning anatomy. The handgun hunter cannot afford to make such a mistake. You must study the proper shot placement, usually just behind the fore leg. You need to study the proper shot placement for an animal that is squared to you or facing away from you. I have done so, and it is amazing how often a heavy bone will obstruct the heart. I have practiced for shots I have never had to make. The more you study these problems the more you will be inclined toward more practice and the heavy, deep-penetration calibers.

THE MAGNUM CALIBERS

There are five useful standard Magnum calibers. These are the .22 Magnum, the .32 H&R Magnum, the .357 Magnum, the .41 Magnum, and the .44 Magnum. I could get along quite well with the .22 Magnum and the .44 Magnum, but the others have merit. All may be brilliantly accurate. The .22 Magnum is a real crackerjack of a round with great potential. I prefer not to overmatch the cartridge, but the .22 Magnum has a reputation for killing out of proportion to its size. The .357 is among my favorite cartridges. With the .44 Magnum, I respect the power of this round but admit I do not fire it often for recreation. These are wonderful handgun cartridges well suited to recreational and practical use.

CHAPTER 14

Personal Defense

I WEAR A SIDEARM OR HAVE one at arm's reach most of the day. I have done so for most of my adult life. I am not afraid or paranoid, but I am aware of what our criminal class is capable of. The depredations and perversions of our protein-fed ex-con criminal class are frightening when viewed from afar and far more so when they are in your face. When the lips are bared to the green teeth and the wart hairs quiver, they may be stopped only by a determined person willing to use force. The handgun is the logical defensive choice.

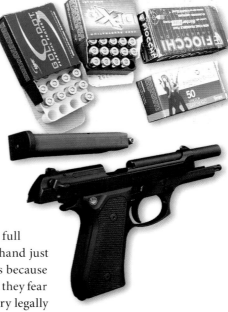

The handgun is readily concealed and may be brought into action quickly. The handgun is feared by some because it may be concealed but that is its worth to the citizen. In my experience criminals are not always armed. There is always the punk or those full of posture but most take the gun in hand just before they commit the crime. This is because criminals are known to the police and they fear searches and pat downs. Since we carry legally with a permit, we have no such fear. (At least in the free states we carry a permit; the people's republics that prevent concealed carry are another matter.) Law-abiding citizens carry to save their

What matters the most in a combat pistol is reliability. The author's M 9 Beretta is a reliable handgun that has never malfunctioned.

lives and for no other reason. But the criminal has the advantage because he knows he is going to attack. We have only reaction.

Criminals take away our dignity and some part of our humanity when they rob or intimidate us. Those citizens who resist a criminal's violent attack are far more likely to survive. Those who are docile are treated to viscous attacks. When it comes to the more serious crimes such as takeover robberies and home invasions, there must be a plan in place to counter such a threat. Reaction and training may not be enough to overcome numbers and the criminal element's determination.

Personal defense is a human right, but today many human rights are reduced to something called civil rights. Civil rights are fine as a concept, but they are often misunderstood. Civil rights are not granted to us by fiat but because of the concerted actions of citizens to earn these rights. These rights, including the right to keep and bear arms, have been bought and paid for with blood. These rights are to be respected by all people and for all people. I am trained in many disciplines including the knife, rifle, shotgun, and open hand. I have traveled to other countries when my primary means of defense was my wits.

During my time in a police uniform I experienced several difficulties, including one that gave my face a look similar to a rock quarry that has been dynamited. My trigger finger has been broken and I have other permanent scars. I am a grown man and weigh more than two hundred pounds. I was in my prime when most of these fights occurred. I can only shudder at the thoughts of what might have happened to an elderly person or a child in a similar situation. All I was doing was getting in the way of criminal mischief.

This is a book about handguns, and handguns is what I teach, but do not allow the handgun to be your only tool. Work on your physical conditioning and learn intermediate measures of personal defense.

TRAINING FOR PERSONAL DEFENSE

In many sports the rule is no pain no gain. When you are attempting to learn the pistol you may be using muscles you have not used before in handgun training. We put aside other pursuits and attempt to master the handgun.

The author demonstrates the Weaver stance. Note the angles represented in the shadow on the range construct.

When personal defense is a real need rather than an abstract concept, the heat is on to learn the handgun. If you are a serious student you will not begrudge the time spent on the range. The reward is competence with an implement that few truly master. Even if you are primarily a competition shooter you wish to be all you can be, and the personal-defense disciplines relate to competition.

You must have a rational organization of training. Too long a training session at the range may be counterproductive. You may see your skills deteriorate rather than build. You must adhere to the proper training steps and doctrine that works. We must follow the proper doctrine or code of conduct to avoid becoming a will-o'-the-wisp that moves with every new idea. The basics will always carry you through any type of competition or other difficulty. Develop a personal training style and remain true to the fundamentals but remain open to new tactics and new ideas. This dedication prepares us for action whether it's an IDPA match or defense against a psychopathic killer. You must engage the handgun systematically and regularly. Some talk while others walk the walk and others rely upon skills they cannot demonstrate. Due diligence in mastering the handgun prepares us for those difficult chores that come up from time to time.

As you strive to control the handgun you will be breaking open a shell of understanding. I am not speaking of the pain of blistered palms and bruises or muscle aches, but muscles do become tired and the movements required in mastering the handgun are demanding. In training individuals to use the handgun I have detected great differences in attitude and motivation. Some do not appreciate discipline but are disdainful of anything that requires great effort. These shooters won't prosper in anything they attempt unless they change their mindset.

We all begin in the same place. I think that the single most common shortcoming of students is a lack of gunhandling skills. Purchasing a handgun no more makes one an expert than buying a boat makes you a harbor pilot. You do not prove skill by ownership but by mastering the piece and by demonstration. If you think you will rise to the occasion during a gunfight you are a greater optimist than Tony Robbins. The essential elements of marksmanship are the same whatever the discipline. The proper sight picture, trigger control, stance, and grip must be learned. You really need the NRA basic handgun course.

If you need a shooting coach, find one. Search the National Rifle Association website for coaches. Many shooters, including myself, are self-taught, but it is probably the harder road. I learned to shoot through distance education. My grandfather taught me the safety basics. I believe that once you have the basic NRA course under your belt you can become a good shot on your own, but that basic handgun course is vital. Get the right material and learn the basic components of marksmanship. Practice in earnest. The handgun may be your lifeline.

THE STANCE

The foundation of all shooting skills is the stance, both literally and figuratively. I prefer the stance known as the weaver stance. When preparing to shoot we need to be in a braced position with our legs about shoulder-width apart. The weight of the body should be on the front leg primarily. The knees are slightly flexed, and the body is bladed toward the target. The strong-side hand grasps the handgun and the weak-side arm is slightly bent in supporting the firing hand. To assume the weaver stance, the strong-side hand is extended as far as possible. The weak-side hand grasps the strong side and draws the strong side back until the arm of the support side is slightly bent. The weaver is not the only stance that works well, but for most of us it will provide the most stable firing platform.

This is the isosceles, basically thrusting the handgun in front of the body. This is a simple stance that works well enough.

The isosceles stance is simpler and is accomplished by thrusting the arms forward. There are tradeoffs. The weaver may interfere with some types of movement, such as moving along a wall, but the weaver is more easily used to transverse toward the shooter's weak side. The isosceles is easier to learn quickly. Either works well for the dedicated shooter. Whichever stance you use, the principles of marksmanship are the same. I have found the weaver is the more stable platform and absorbs recoil better.

Study the chapter on marksmanship. The firing grip and trigger compression learned during marksmanship training will be your guide in personal-defense shooting. The difference is the time frame. You are required to draw and fire in a compressed time frame. You will be attempting to control a powerful handgun. The handgun may be as light and powerful as you are able to carry. Controlling this type of handgun demands practice in controlling the handgun and absolute attention to detail.

When firing quickly you have to realize that even though the trigger compression is taken more quickly, you cannot jerk the trigger. The trigger is pressed quickly to the rear but smoothly without jerking. It is possible to miss at close ranges and the cause will be a lack of trigger control. The surprise break is essential. Press the trigger to the rear until it breaks and allow the trigger to reset. Remember the most common mistake: Too many shooters linger too long on the sight picture and realize they are running out of time and need to break the shot. They then jerk the trigger. Slow down if you need to in order to be certain you have a hit, but don't get flustered and jerk the trigger. This ensures a miss.

COMBAT SHOOTING

Interpersonal combat is unwelcome and unexpected but sometimes forced upon us. Formulating a plan to survive in an action that requires a decision to be made in a split second is a daunting proposition. You must have the requisite mental drive to do what you must do. Some have been brought up in a passive background and may not be willing to admit that society has degenerated. To some this degeneration has meant a loss of position and to others a loss of safety. To me it means that dangerous individuals are more prevalent than ever. The danger exists and only good luck or a miracle will save the unskilled. If you are concerned with the welfare of your family, then you need to have the means available of meeting an unanticipated attack. I hope to illuminate you with my experience and accumulated education.

I have seen many outrages perpetrated by the criminal element, but I have to transcend my own thoughts and emotions and present only reliable data. In all of my research the persuasive warning knell is present. There is almost always a precipitating action that warns us an attack is coming. That is the warning that if heeded allows us to escape. The warning of an eminent fight is the whistle on the range; on the street it may be "I need your money."

Action beats reaction. After years of practice I have come to believe that reaction time may be cut by diligent practice. Situational awareness, being aware of your surroundings, is a valuable asset. You must evaluate your physical ability. If you are out of shape then some techniques will not work for you. A force evaluation of how you are able to deal with a threat should be included before you prepare to train. Next, let's look at some of the best training moves.

The stance, firing grip, trigger compression, sight alignment, and sight picture are the fundamentals of marksmanship. These are not tactics. Tactics are moves designed to give you an advantage. You can do well in most forms of competition and in hunting without a fast presentation from the holster. But the fast presentation—presentation being presenting the handgun to the target—is essential to combat pistol craft. The draw is simple enough, simply bringing the handgun out of the holster. That's fine, and you can draw the handgun pretty quickly with practice. But the complete presentation involves drawing the handgun, coming into the firing stance, and addressing the target. When you begin training you will be drawing from a holster on the belt without any covering garment. Once you have reached a certain stage of proficiency—when you do not make mistakes on the draw—you will move to the concealed-carry draw.

This military intelligence officer has had the opportunity to study several gunfights of the Old West. Tools change, people do not.

The practice of attending IDPA matches is a wonderful training ground as IDPA demands that you draw from concealed carry. When you wear one of the covering vests that are usually worn at these events, the draw is practiced as follows: You clear the covering garment in a practiced hand movement to the rear with the hand moving under the garment. Sweep the hand below the handgun as the elbow shoots to the rear. The draw must represent economy of motion. Do not move the hand to the holstered handgun, take a grip, and then draw. That is terribly slow. The hand moves to the pistol and scoops it out in one smooth motion. The next step in accepted form is for the shooting hand to meet the support hand in front of the navel, affirm the grip, and bring the handgun forward into a shooting stance. If done correctly, this action takes place in about a second. A practiced hand should be able to draw and fire and get a center hit on a man-sized target at ten yards in 1.5 seconds. This happens all of the time on a stationary range. Many of my students are pretty slick with the presentation, but combat is different.

This is a modified weaver, with the body facing the opponent and with less blading than the original weaver. This means a lot if you wear a bulletproof vest.

We are not interested in shooting-school instruction but tactical-school instruction at this point. You have mastered the fundamentals and now you have learned to quickly present the handgun from concealed carry. Now comes the nitty-gritty part: hitting an assailant. It is quite a bit different from firing at a paper target. Sometimes the range is short, sometimes not, but the best information indicates that the average personal-defense incident occurs inside of seven yards or twenty-one feet. When you study the paper and consider the likely scenarios, the term "bad breath range" comes to mind. This type of action demands a different discipline than target shooting.

Adopting a dueling stance or bull's-eye stance will get you killed quickly. The boxer's stance we have mentioned is ideal for balance and for controlling a handgun's recoil. If you adopt the weaver stance you have to be ready to quickly move into it and move tactically. If you have not mastered getting into the weaver quickly and are having a hard time of it, then the isosceles is better. You have to gauge your own skill and practice constantly to eliminate excess or unnecessary movement. You may have to decide in each situation if you should fire with one hand or two. At short range you will wish to blade your body toward the opponent and protect your draw. He may be almost on top of you.

The adversary may be close enough to interfere with the draw or even to gain control of the handgun. You have to consider each scenario. Do not be caught unprepared and freeze up in indecision. I guarantee you this will happen if you have not practiced a wide variety of tactics and if you are not competent in gunhandling.

At this time we need to pause and consider the great lessons of the past and give praise to the National Rifle Association. Without the NRA, there would probably be no police training or at the least police training would be very poor. The NRA was behind the original Hogan's Alley later adopted by the FBI. The NRA really got pistol shooting going as far as competition goes. Of course, stylized events such as bull's-eye shooting had nothing to do with combat shooting. The NRA

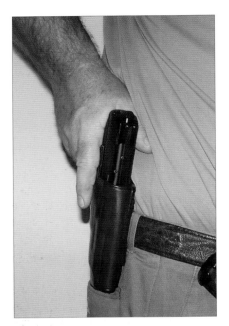

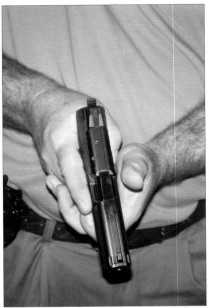

The author is practicing scooping his HK 9mm from an Alessi holster. With practice, the movement is second nature.

The hands meet in front of the belt buckle, and you are ready to present the handgun to the target. Practice is vital.

developed credible training. Combat practice was slow to evolve, but today we have excellent resources.

One thing we must discuss is point shooting, or instinctive shooting. Every so often, someone introduces ideas about point shooting in a magazine article or from a speaker's podium. I am certain that one reason point shooting was advocated is because early handguns had poor sights. You couldn't use the sights because you couldn't see them. Today we have no such excuse. True instinctive shooting is a different matter. I would never teach students not to use their sights. Always use your sights and take a proper sight picture no matter how close the range if possible. The problem is that sometimes it isn't possible to acquire a good sight picture. There must be alternative techniques.

Hip shooting isn't viable unless the assailant has you by the throat or is stabbing you. Then it works if you are on the same level and you are able to jam the gun into his body. Otherwise the handgun is brought to the eyes to sight. Here is where some most interesting fast techniques come into play and the sights are used. Colonel Rex Applegate developed a shooting technique based on the writing and action of the great gunfighters of the past. The shortcoming of these techniques was that they were most useful inside twelve feet or so. That's fine; practice using the Applegate at very short range and be certain you take a better aim at longer range.

The Applegate program is not to ignore the sights, far from it. But they are range-sensitive. At short range the technique it to focus on the target. Focus on the area that you wish the bullets to strike and keep the handgun just under eye level. Fire a double tap. I am not crazy. Believe me, this technique works at a few feet. The top of the pistol slide or the top strap of a revolver is your aiming point. The Applegate point is another technique that is useful at close range.

Applegate taught the Applegate point by holding the handgun by the side of the body and taking a step forward. I incorporate a draw into this technique. Draw the handgun from the holster and present the handgun toward the target. As you step forward you are giving your body an excellent platform for support. You look at the target and focus on the area you wish to strike. Shoot as soon as the front sight breaks the plane between your eyes and the target fire. You may be surprised at the results you will have with this technique. When training time is precious this is a technique that gets shooters up and running with some skill quickly. Remember, I am not advocating not using your sights. I am advocating using only the front sight in a desperate short-range tactic.

There are many other considerations in personal defense. An important tactic is to find cover as soon as possible. If you have enough time or warning get to cover. You will have to decide in an instant if you should draw or take cover, as the two conflict with the other. Once you have cover you will have a great advantage. Another good tactic is to get out of the line of fire. Simply step to one side as you draw. Be in the habit of redirecting the line of force. For ranges of three yards and longer you should lock into a two-hand hold and fire as accurately as possible. There is some discussion of the exact point of aim we should take. I never counsel

the student to fire for the whole body; rather, pick out a finite spot on the body and fire. Area aiming will result in misses. The area of center mass is not the center of the upper chest but the center of the mass of the whole body, and this is not the best aiming point. The upper chest is the better area. The proper term is "center of mass," not center mass, and they are actually different terms.

Some of you reading this are professionals, and you realize the level of practice that goes into acquiring marksmanship. You practice until you cannot

The original Weaver stance is a solid firing platform. The recoil of the LW Springfield .45 is controlled by this stance.

make a mistake. The primary focus in a critical incident is to quickly incapacitate the adversary. The only reason you have to fire, morally or legally, is because the attacker's actions are so terrible he must be stopped. It must not matter if he expires as a result of being stopped, but this is immaterial. We fire to stop not to kill. You must have paid attention in training or you cannot rise to the occasion and will be operating below normal capacity.

When training with people of every stripe I find that there is often a disharmony in definition. Accuracy and marksmanship are confused. Accuracy is mechanical and may be demonstrated by a trained shooter. Marksmanship is not firing little groups. Groups never saved a life. Marksmanship is hitting the target on demand. The radial dispersion of a ten-round group on the target is worthy of our interest if we are target shooting, but the one good hit is what a combat shooter strives for. At the range you know how the targets are placed. The range is known beforehand. The target is not moving or obscured. You fire at the whistle command. There is really no excuse for a miss in this type of environment. You have done everything, consciously or not, to stack the odds in your favor.

Center of mass, sometimes erroneously referred to as center mass, is an aiming point and must be understood. Hitting somewhere is better than hitting nowhere, but the center of mass shot is preferred. Even better is a deliberate choice to fire for the arterial region. The strong .45 and the weak .38 are more alike than they differ when compared to a shotgun or center-fire rifle, and shot placement is the best multiplier of force. The proper aiming point is the upper third of the torso, dead center in this mass. This is the heart and arterial region. There is no other shot that will incapacitate an adversary for certain. Cranial shots are discouraged due to their difficulty and unreliable results—bullets skid off the round oglive of the skull. The center of mass shot is your aiming point.

Consider the placement of the target on the range. You often place the target where it is easy to address. Fire a few times at a target that is partially obscured. Center of mass also comes into play in this type of aiming. If only the leg or the foot or the arm or the handgun is exposed, fire at the center of the visible mass for the greatest likelihood of a hit. Aiming for the edge of the target will often result in a miss. When the target is not obscured, the upper torso is the best target. If your shot is not perfect, but your life is in danger, take the shot.

A raking shot, which is difficult to practice on a paper target, rakes across the maximum length or width of the body. This type of shot is often very effective, particularly if it hits bone. A shot in the lower body isn't a stopping shot, but there is considerable evidence that such a hit is painful and may end the fight quickly. Hit the adversary, hit them quickly, and keep hitting them until they are no longer a threat.

SHOOTING ON THE MOVE

Practiced shooters have a great advantage if they are able to shoot and move. It isn't easy, but it's not rocket science, as in hitting the moon. We aim a rocket at where

When firing at short range the one-hand grip is useful, but must be practiced for acceptable results.

the moon will be, not at where it is the day the rocket is launched. Some shooters practice hitting moving targets with the shotgun with some success, but there is practically no correction in short-range pistol shooting.

At combat ranges the problem is not difficult. If the adversary is moving simply, keep the front sight on him and fire. If he is really running and firing at you, he is unlikely to hit you, but at short range he may hit you by sheer luck. Put the sights on him at the outer edge of his body in the direction he is running. No more lead is needed. Do not jerk the trigger, but press it and keep moving as you fire. Do not fire and jerk. Move smoothly with the target, fire, and keep moving after you have fired in an uninterrupted motion. A side-stepping drill is also worth your attention. A drill I practice often is to draw, side step, and then move to one side while firing at the target. In time you will become adept at putting lead into the target. Always let safety be your guide.

The tactics mentioned will handle 99 percent of the problems you will encounter. Marksmanship will carry the day. Practice simple drills such as drawing and firing at a man-sized target at ten yards. Get the hit in one and a half seconds or less. Practice the presentation relentlessly. The presentation leads into the firing stance and into the proper sight acquisition. It is most vital you get the technique right.

THE PRESENTATION

To present the handgun to the target, the elbow shoots to the rear and the hand drops below the holster mouth then scoops the handgun out of the holster. The hands meet in front of the belt buckle and force the handgun forward toward the target. The sights are acquired and the handgun is fired. It is as simple as that. Practice, practice, and practice more.

Taking a step forward, the author brings his Walther 9mm to eye level and fires. This is a good short-range tactic that gets hits quickly.

SELECTING A PERSONAL-DEFENSE HANDGUN

I can no more choose the perfect handgun for your needs than choose your spouse, but I can make recommendations. Your personal comfort level and lifestyle must be considered. Just the same, there is a minimal level of protection that experienced shooters are comfortable with, and these are the .38 Special and 9mm Luger calibers. I cannot and will not recommend any caliber less than these two for personal defense. Anyone who recommends a smaller caliber needs a reality check. I realize the light .380s and .32s are popular, and a few of the better designs even function well, most of the time. But I am not willing to lose my life because I sought a few ounces of comfort.

I have recommended the minimum calibers, but beyond this recommendation the field is confusing. Should the choice be a revolver or an automatic? The main drawback of the revolver is related to firepower, which is a perceived fault as much as a real shortcoming. The revolver is the simplest and most reliable type. Do not let a tactical hypochondriac's opinion occlude your vision. When choosing the handgun we must stay in touch with reality and choose a handgun that fits our lifestyle. You must include in the choice an honest assessment of not only the likely scenario you will face but also your own ability. There are some who become emotional over handgun selection and cling to their personal choice with a vengeance. Perhaps they have too much ego invested.

There are essential elements a personal-defense handgun must possess. While the recreational handgun is a lot of fun and it is difficult to find a handgun that will not amuse you in some way, the personal-defense handgun has a more serious mission. You must think things out before you purchase.

The handgun is carried to allow the user to gain control of a situation and to survive that situation. Given a handgun of adequate power, the more ergonomic the handgun and the better it handles the more your chances of quickly bringing the handgun into action and performing efficiently. There is a saying among IPSC shooters that a certain handgun "drives smoothly." This is an apt description. The controls must be well placed for rapid manipulation. The handgun should not be too small or too large. A too small handgun that cramps the hand or thrusts the fingers into the controls in recoil is counter indicated. A too large handgun handles more slowly and is slower into action and difficult to conceal. Conversely, a light and powerful handgun, often chosen by a novice, is best suited to a well trained shooter and practiced individual.

The handgun must be reliable. Reliability is a propensity of the handgun to fire with each press of the trigger. An unreliable handgun is a nuisance that must be discarded. Some makes and types are more reliable than others. Beretta, Browning, Colt, CZ, Glock, Heckler & Koch, Kimber, Para Ordnance, Ruger, SIG SAUER, Springfield, and Smith & Wesson are among the most reliable choices. I think that if there is a shortcoming among modern shooters it is an inability to judge quality. A handgun that has been proven in a rigorous military or police test program and passed with flying colors is always a good choice. The National Institute of Justice sets a minimum standard for reliability and that is firing three hundred rounds between cleanings. That is not a high standard to my idea of a combat handgun, but three hundred trouble-free rounds is a starting place.

You would do well to study those police and military test programs in which the popular service pistols have been vetted. The military test of the Beretta 92 as an example was extensive. The Beretta is proven by any standard. European tests of the Beretta, SIG, and CZ pistols are also verifiable. The Ohio State Patrol fired 228,000 rounds of ammunition during their search for a service pistol. A SIG product, the P226, was the single most reliable handgun. Many handguns are far less proven and many have had problematical debuts.

The handgun must be accurate enough for the task at hand. Some handguns are more accurate than others, but almost any quality handgun will place the magazine or cylinder of ammunition into a single ragged hole at seven yards. There are two components of accuracy: practical accuracy and intrinsic accuracy. Practical accuracy, how the handgun handles with the shooter firing off their hind legs, is the most important. Most shooters fail to realize the short time involved in a defensive situation. You need to get the handgun out, get a hit, and be certain the first hit counts. Intrinsic accuracy is the mechanical accuracy a handgun is capable of in perfect conditions from a machine rest. It's interesting that intrinsic accuracy has little bearing upon combat handgun selection.

The handgun should be powerful enough to incapacitate the aggressor with a minimum of well directed rounds. This means at least the 9mm or .38 as discussed. The better choice is a .357 Magnum revolver or the .45-caliber automatic. These two are proven, produce excellent wound ballistics, and are controllable with practice. The 10mm automatic, the .40 S&W, .44 Special, and .45 Colt are acceptable. When you are choosing the handgun, the best route is to shoot them all. There are a number of indoor ranges that offer excellent facilities and handguns for rental.

While it can be expensive to rent one firearm after the other, this is less expensive than trading constantly and purchasing a handgun that is not suitable for your ability or needs. Give each an honest try. In this situation, the pressure is off. You did not purchase the handgun, and you do not have to live with it if you do not like it. You will probably enjoy the experience and move closer toward the final choice. But do not simply fire the handgun in target-style shooting. Challenge both the shooter and the handgun. Fire a variety of one-hand shoulder-point drills at seven yards, two-hand rapid-fire at ten yards, and various speed drills. You will find that all handguns are not created equal. There will be a certain handgun that suits your shooting style and which you find most effective in your hands.

Choosing the handgun isn't just about range work. It is about handling the handgun. Does the pistol have sharp edges? Does the frame gouge your hand? Are you able to quickly present the handgun from your concealed-carry holster? Does the handgun fit your hand, handle well, and come into action quickly. Are you comfortable with the handgun in its ready mode? Do you like the simplicity of the Glock? Do you prefer a handgun with a positive manual safety? Do you prefer the long double-action first-shot press of the double-action SIG P220? Is the simplicity of the revolver immensely appealing?

Keeping the eye on the target, the author draws and prepares to address the threat.

CHOICES IN PERSONAL-DEFENSE HANDGUNS

Over the years I have handled every type of handgun and quite a few examples of individual design. There are modern types that are excellent examples of the gunmakers' art, and there are handguns that are produced as cheaply as possible. A good shot may make up for some of the shortcomings of an inferior handgun, but who wishes to deploy an inferior handgun?

When the subject of a good, cheap 1911 comes up, I often feel like asking the person making the comment if he would like a good cheap Corvette! (Do not remind me of the Opel GT.) I feel for my cash-strapped brothers and sisters, but quality can be expensive. For those on a strict budget, the Glock is readily available and is probably the most reliable of the low-bid handguns. Within its limitations the Glock is a good service pistol. I would prefer a

Glock over a cheap copy of the Glock or one of the inexpensive 1911 knock-offs. By the same token I would prefer a good used Smith & Wesson revolver to a clone gun. Buy quality. I could get by easily with my Smith & Wesson revolvers and quality 1911-type handguns, but here is a short list of some of the best choices.

Beretta 92

I keep Berettas on hand because I train military personnel. I learned long ago it is best to train people well and not criticize their gear. I am not happy the military is strapped with a small-bore pistol, but the M9 or Beretta 92 is a good handgun outside the limitations of the caliber. I am impressed with the quality of fit and finish and the reliability of the Beretta. The pistol is among the most reliable ever built. Muzzle flip is light, recoil mild, and accuracy good to outstanding. The long double-action trigger may be learned with practice. The handling and safety features are good. The Beretta is not a heavy-duty pistol that will last for 100,000 rounds as a quality 1911 will, but you could do worse than choosing the Beretta.

An example of a new convert to the Beretta 92 is my buddy Jerry, who lives close to the Tex-Mex border. Not long ago a gang stole a truck and rammed it into Jerry's shop. Since this happened at midnight, no one was injured, but Jerry's shop suffered thousands of dollars worth of damage. The twenty-thousand-dollar truck they had stolen was totaled. The gang escaped with perhaps a thousand dollars worth of leather goods. Nearby security cameras showed that four men were involved. Like myself, Jerry had packed a 1911 .45 most of his life, and when in the field used a .357 Magnum revolver. He now wears a Beretta 92 9mm and two spare magazines everywhere he goes. With forty-six rounds of +P+ 9mm on tap, he is well armed against gangs. He can empty the magazine into a man-sized silhouette at seven yards in just a few seconds and reload in two seconds flat. There is something to high capacity, good control, and flawless reliability.

SIG P Series

My personal favorite SIG is the P220, a .45-caliber variant. The double-action trigger press of the SIG is smooth and the frame-mounted decocker is easily manipulated. The pistol is very accurate. SIGARMS pistols are among the most reliable ever built. The new SIG P250 is at present my first choice among the modern double-action–only pistol types. The trigger is smooth and the pistols are controllable. While I prefer blue steel and walnut, it would be foolish not to admit that the P250 is a great pistol.

My friend Todd Randall Parker is a true adherent of the SIG and feels that the P229 is among the best handling and most accurate SIG pistols. Everywhere I go I find professionals with an eye for quality using the SIG pistol in one of the many variants. I cannot fault the choice. As another good friend Catherine often points out, when the brass (police administrators) purchases the SIG, the troopers know that the brass did not go with the low bid and purchased a quality pistol.

Glock

The Glock is now everyman's pistol and holds three quarters of the police market in this country. It is true that this is largely based on the low bid, but there is something to the Glock. It is reliable, accurate enough for most chores, and easily maintained. It is the Q ship of pistols. The shooter is the most important part of the equation. Learn the Glock trigger action well and cling to this pistol and no other. Always be cognizant of the lack of a manual safety. There have been too many troublesome discharges of the Glock in which shooters have been injured, but the fact is true safety is between the ears. In the hands of the good guys and girls the Glock is stopping bad guys every day. My personal concealed-carry favorite is the Glock Model 36, the single-column thin-grip .45. I have also used several of the .45 GAP versions with good results.

Smith & Wesson

The Smith & Wesson M&P automatic has superior handfit to the Glock, and the option of a manual safety is a big advantage. The biggest advantage is the fact that the M&P fits most hands well even in the large .45-caliber size. The .45-caliber Glock is too large and bulky for most hand sizes. Smith & Wesson has scored a home run in design with this pistol. They have an uphill fight against the Glock. The M&P is not designed to compete with the SIG or Beretta or a 1911 but with the Glock. They are doing a good job of it. My friend Doyle carries a Smith & Wesson M&P compact 9mm and is well pleased with the fit, reliability, and performance.

1911 Handguns

There are a number of expensive custom 1911 handguns that are worth their price. Foremost among these are the superb pistols from Wilson Combat. The Les Baer line is another source of first-class gun steel. When it comes to everyday working 1911 handguns Colt, Kimber, and Springfield are good choices. It is a good rule not to purchase the low end—the GI versions—or the most expensive such as the Springfield Professional. The pistols in the middle seem to strike the best balance of features and affordability for most shooters.

The Kimber CDP and Gold Combat line are particularly attractive. Kimber's quality control is European in scope. The Kimber 1911 is often compared to the SIG P series in a favorable manner. The Kimber probably has the Europeans beat. The 1911 pistols are offered with modern features including ambidextrous safety levers, self-luminous iron sights, and light rails. The Springfield LW Operator is a particular favorite for those who favor rail guns and combat lights. There is no handgun faster to an accurate first-shot hit than a 1911 when the pistol is properly carried cocked and locked. The 1911 types virtually rule every form of competition. The pistol is proven in extensive operations and remains the most reliable hard-use pistol for long-term use, with quite a few in service with well over fifty thousand rounds on the frame. While the 1911 is not for everyone be certain you have a good reason to discount the pistol.

Heckler & Koch

I find the HK USP too large and bulky. I do not like the handling. The HK P30 is another matter. I have never handled a nicer shooting pistol. The decocker has erroneously been criticized, but the P30 features a tactically minded decocker that will never be accessed accidentally. The P30 is well worth your investigation.

Revolvers

Smith & Wesson has produced the world's finest double-action revolvers for more than one hundred years. The revolvers are neatly classified in the J-frame, the smallest type, typically a five-shot .38; the K-frame, a six-shot .38 or .357; the L-frame, a six- or seven-shot .357; and the N-frame, a six- or eight-shot .357 or a six-shot .41-, .44- or .45-caliber. Smith & Wesson revolvers are well made of good material and demonstrate Yankee craftsmanship.

While the new style revolvers look considerably different in detail than earlier versions, the modern revolvers are the most accurate and reliable ever made. The J-frame 442 with humpback frame and concealed hammer is probably the ideal choice for most of us in the snub-nose line. The K-frame six shooters are among the best-balanced and fast-handling revolvers ever made. The N-frame revolvers are larger and more difficult to handle quickly; however, once the N-frame is out of the holster and in the hand it offers a very stable firing platform. The .44 Magnum is really too much for personal defense, unless large animals are a part of the threat. The N-frame .357 Magnum with heavy loads is a great choice for home defense or trekking in the wild.

Taurus

Taurus is a full line company that offers a selection of everything, from revolvers to 1911 handguns. Taurus revolvers are defending homes across America, helping cash-strapped working people with a handgun well worth its modest price. The Model 85 .38 Special is an excellent choice. This five-shot .38 features a smooth-action, good sights, and a heavy underlugged barrel. The various K-frame six-shot revolvers are well balanced carry guns. My personal favorite among the Taurus pistols is the Tracker series of revolvers. Offering good balance and handfit, they are well suited to most personal-defense needs.

PART IV

Maintenance and Customization

CHAPTER 15

Taking Care of Your Handgun

WHEN YOU CONSIDER MAINTENANCE REQUIREMENTS, remember that revolvers and automatics differ considerably. You need more mechanical aptitude to maintain the revolver. Keeping the handgun clean must be addressed, otherwise you will destroy accuracy. As an example, if you have been using good-quality cast bullets as I do from Accu Cast, Dardas, Magnus, Moyers, Montana Bullet Works, Oregon Trail, or a few reputable manufacturers, you will not experience a severe problem with leading unless you neglect cleaning after firing thousands of rounds of ammunition.

If we clean the barrel every five hundred rounds or so, the worst problems will be avoided. The best bet is to use the brush until there are no lead deposits seen on the white patch. I have been using the triangular patches from Rigel Products with excellent results. If you use copper bullets there will be light copper deposits. In either case, the cleaning program is the same.

These are very similar handguns, the Beretta M9 and the Walther P1. Each strips down in nearly identical fashion and neither is difficult to maintain. Note the recoil spring of the Beretta 92 at full uncompressed length.

Blue Wonder Gun Blue is essential for touching up small scratches. There is little reason to take the pistol to a gunsmith for minor work.

The Beretta and Walther pistols use an oscillating wedge for lockup. The Walther pistol on the bottom has had the wedge replaced. The locking block has been known to crack, so keep your eyes on this piece.

To begin cleaning the revolver I use a copper brush for leading, then a cotton cleaning patch soaked in Hoppes, and finally I run a clean patch through the bore. There are tips that will help ensure that the revolver is properly cleaned. A used toothbrush is a great aid in scrubbing powder ash out of the top strap area and other hard-to-reach areas. The blind mortises of some handguns are difficult to clean, and a toothbrush is the best tool I have found. A good aerosol spray works well as long as it is allowed to dry well before the handgun is loaded again. Some aerosols will penetrate to the primer and render the priming compound inert. These aerosols are designed to penetrate, and they do so very well. Be certain to dry the slide and breech face after using an aerosol. A dud round is a hard pill to swallow during a critical incident. When you are cleaning do not ignore the firing-pin channel. A clogged firing pin channel will prevent proper operation of the firing pin and result in erratic accuracy. Sometimes an aerosol scrub works in the firing pin channel, but I have also used a pick or a .22-caliber cleaning rod to clear the channel. Transfer bar actions are immune from this problem, and also seem to handle high-pressure Magnum cartridges in a superior manner. Finally, dry the handgun and wipe off the surface. If the handgun is to be stored, I like to add a light coat of lubricating oil on the exposed surfaces, but if it is ready for action I forgo this step.

AUTOMATICS

Once the automatic has been cleared of all ammunition and the magazine and chamber have been checked, I lock the slide to the rear. The next step is to turn the take-down lever down to allow the slide to run off of the frame in the case of the SIG, Beretta, Luger, or similar pistol. The Glock demands the utmost care in disassembly as the take-down levers are each pressed down at the same time and the trigger is pressed to be certain the action is decocked. Keep your fingers away from the muzzle!

This procedure is more complicated with the 1911 types. You begin by cleaning the pistol of any ammunition. Next, you move the barrel bushing to one side to allow the spring cap to be removed while making certain the spring cap does not take flight. Some pistols will demand a barrel bushing wrench be used to remove the bushing. This is usually true of tightly fitted pistols such as the Les Baer. Once the spring cap is removed spring pressure is alleviated. Next, the slide is locked to the rear and the slide lock lined up with the witness hole in the frame. The slide stop, or slide lock as it is also called, is then pressed out to the left. The slide is then moved forward and off of the frame. The slide and recoil guide are lifted out of the slide and placed to one side.

This is a simplistic description of typical locked-breech service-type pistols. With the blowback pistol the most common take-down sequence is to bring the slide to the rear and lift it upward and forward off of the fixed barrel. The Walther PPK requires that you unhinge the trigger guard, while the Bersa features a takedown latch similar to the Beretta pistols. The Astra Constable, as one example, features a pair of Glock like take-down levers. The recoil spring of these handguns wraps around the barrel. Other types have their own peculiarities. A general description is fine for our purposes, but you really need to study the owner's manual and if possible the NRA disassembly books. There are several NRA guides available. All books and manuals by J. B. Wood on this subject are first-class resources.

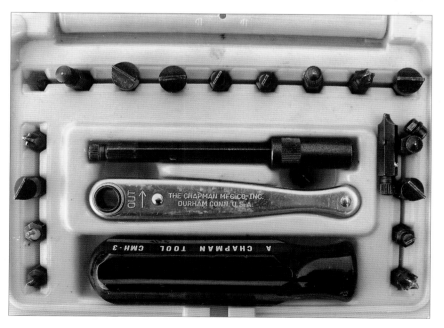

This is the Chapman Gunsmith's toolkit. This is an essential part of every handgunner's kit.

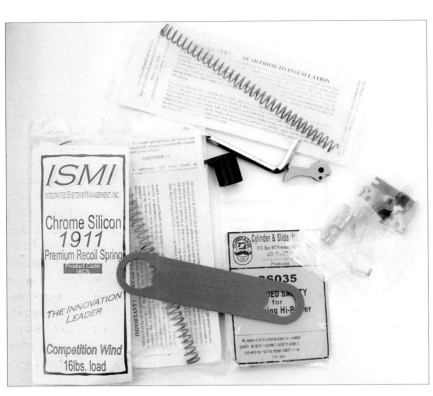

A few spare parts from Apex for the Webley revolver: ISMI springs for the 1911 and a bushing wrench are just part of the author's kit. A working knowledge of the handgun is very desirable.

Among the easiest of all handguns to maintain is the Glock. This pistol is durable, functionally simple, and easily field stripped.

An advantage of the automatic is that it may be cleaned from the breech end. This allows the user to be certain the chamber as well as the bore is clean. I run a bore brush through the barrel several times, alternating between a brush and a cloth to be certain every trace of lead and copper fouling is removed. You may as well do it right the first time. I also use a brush to remove powder fouling that has found its way into the feed ramp and around the action. Even though I am certain my 1911 pistols, the Beretta M9, and the SIG will go many thousands of rounds with complete reliability, I am also aware that a single piece of foreign material may bring operation to a halt.

Once the pistol is clean you need to think about lubrication. I have seen quite a few failures to function as a result of poor lubrication. Even cops who clean their handgun religiously do not always lubricate the piece properly. The long bearing surfaces where the slide meets the frame need to be lubricated. The barrel needs a drop of oil where it meets the slide, and the cocking block should also be lightly lubricated. If the lubricant is running off of the handgun, then you have used too much. If you are planning a long-range session more lubrication is needed than if you are only lubing for carry use. A few drops in strategic places—the frame rails, the cocking block, and the barrel hood—are all that is needed. The revolver doesn't need much lubrication, but a few drops in the action occasionally keep things going smoothly.

Try to use one of the long applicators to be certain the action is properly lubricated. Beware of a buildup of varnished lubricant in the action of a revolver. Learn how to remove the slide plate properly for detail cleaning of the revolver.

The double-action revolver must be timed correctly. There are also small parts and springs to contend with and a certain level of expertise is demanded.

Few revolvers demand the knowledge of barrel and cylinder gap the Dan Wesson revolver does. These switch-barrel handguns are best reserved for the highly interested.

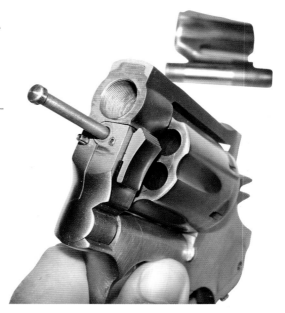

SPECIAL CONSIDERATIONS

If you are living in an environment in which metal surfaces corrode more quickly you may wish to keep a thin film of oil on the metal surfaces. Conversely, a high sand and grit environment demands as little lubrication as possible. A handgun will function for a magazine or so without any lubrication at all, but this is not ideal except in certain harsh environments in which any lubricant draws sand and dust. The same is true of very cold environments such as Alaska. A pistol will not last for fifty rounds on the range without lubrication, but if you are in the sandbox then you need to be as dry as possible.

Some lubricants freeze at very low temperatures. Below zero these lubricants will congeal and make the action sluggish if it functions at all. It is always a good idea to shake the lubricant vigorously before applying. You may notice that oil sometimes separates with long storage and shaking restores the original composition. A number of years ago I conducted a study of lubricants in cold weather. I used a freezer as an artificial test medium. Under carefully controlled conditions I froze not only empty handguns but loaded handguns as well. There were a number of lubricants that passed this rigid test and today I still use RemOil and GunSlick.

I would test any lubricant I planned to bet my life on under similar conditions. It is simple enough to perform a limited test. Pour a little of the lubricant into a bottle cap and let it sit in the freezer overnight. In the morning see if it is still recognizable as a lubricant or if it has frozen. Do not use a loaded firearm. I am a professional and used a controlled environment away from a home. I used the Colt 1911 and Smith & Wesson revolvers in my test and they all passed with flying colors. Another consideration in cold weather is ammunition reliability. I would

This is among the tightest and most accurate handguns the author has used, the CZ P-01. This is a good action and one that requires little maintenance.

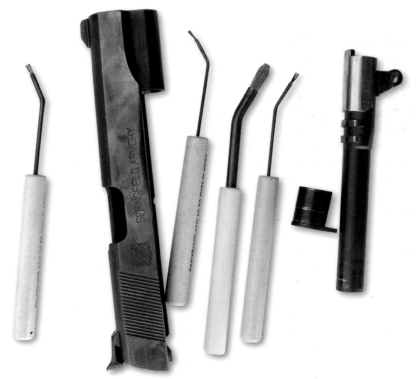

A few simple tools and cleaning gear from Rigel products go a long way. The picks are even better than a toothbrush.

never use anything that is skirting the envelope in pressure. The +P or +P+ loads may rise dangerously in pressure in cold weather. A load already as hot as possible might prove dangerous in such an environment.

SPRING ISSUES

It is recommended that recoil springs and firing pin springs be changed periodically. There are many figures bandied about and the experts seem unable to agree on the length of time and compressions a recoil spring will last. It is SOP to change a service pistol's recoil spring every 5,000 rounds. This rule applies to the Glock, Colt 1911, Beretta 92, and SIG P220. I would change the recoil spring of a short slide pistol such as the Colt Commander or SIG P229 more often. For example, a powerful automatic such as the 10mm Glock is harder on springs than a .45 ACP.

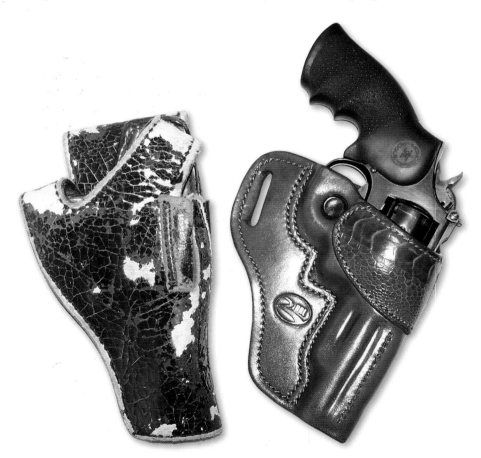

It isn't just the metal that needs maintenance. This holster needs to be discarded after more than a decade of service. The BRL holster on the right should be wiped down with Neet's foot oil occasionally.

When a recoil spring loses a half inch of its free length, it is time to replace it regardless of round count.

Magazines are high-wear items that must be replaced from time to time. I would change the magazine springs every other time I change the recoil spring unless they seem weak before this date. I would change the extractor on the Colt 1911 every 10,000 rounds and the extractor of the CZ 75 type every 8,000 rounds. It may seem like 10,000 rounds of ammunition is a lot of shooting, but I see a lot of high-round handguns. I own several. Revolvers have the advantage of a design that keeps all of the springs relaxed when the revolver is at rest. Just the same, it is not unusual to see a hard-use revolver in need of a hand spring or a mainspring. The bolt sometimes weakens. Often enough a revolver spring fails because the user has clipped the spring to make the action lighter. I would give a service revolver a new set of springs every 10,000 rounds.

FINISH MAINTENANCE

Modern handguns with a quality blue finish or stainless steel handguns are much more resistant to the elements than handguns of a few generations ago although Parkerizing and the now defunct Bunkerizing were pretty durable. A stainless finish encourages the general neglect inherent in some shooters. The handgun must be cleaned after each trip to the range or at least the finish should be wiped

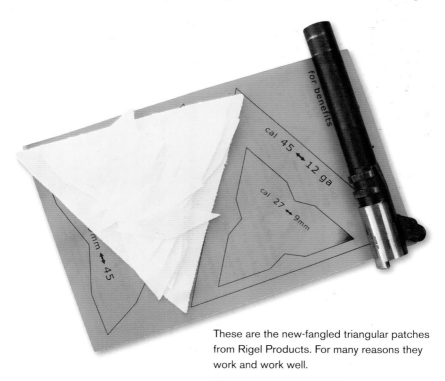

These are the new-fangled triangular patches from Rigel Products. For many reasons they work and work well.

down. Otherwise, corrosion will begin to build a foothold. Even a stainless pistol will pit. They are stain*less* not stain proof.

Some maintenance is practical repair work. While we can replace small parts, a gunsmith is needed to replace or repair dove-tailed sights, hammers, and other major parts. Some of us are able to remove and replace and fit extractors. The most common replacement parts are grip panels. I recently replaced the grip panels of my Webley .455 with an excellent set of reproduction stocks from Gun Parts Corporation. This is a simple operation that is easily done. Replacing springs and repairing magazines is simple once the field-stripping sequence is understood.

If there is any question as to the ability of the shooter to replace the parts, take the handgun to a gunsmith. If you enjoy the game after a time you will become passing fair at replacing parts. The handgun is much like an automobile. Neglect maintenance and repair for a few months and you have a piece of junk on your hands.

CHAPTER 16

Materials and Finishes

HANDGUNS HAVE BEEN PRODUCED FROM iron, steel, brass, and healthy portions of nickel silver. Zinc, aluminum, and scandium have been used to make the pistol lighter. Even ceramics have been used. Polymer frames are the standard for low-bid police handguns. Today, the slides and barrels of handguns are manufactured from high-quality steel or some type of stainless-steel alloy. The frames are a different story with a good mix of cast, aluminum, and polymer popular. But nothing is as strong as forged steel. That is the bottom line. Everything else is either lighter or cheaper or easier to machine into a tool. Even grades of steel differ. Forgings and castings each have adherents. There are advantages to each material.

You may sometimes read that castings may have bubbles or voids in them from the casting process. Cracks and terrible flaws are feared. I am not a trained metallurgist by any means, but just the same I have studied the subject and speak from experience. The modern cast frame if done correctly is as strong as any. After all, aren't the handguns we generally consider the strongest in the world—Ruger revolvers—produced by casting?

Smith & Wesson is a showcase for different materials. The Smith & Wesson .45 automatic, top, features a steel slide with special coating and a polymer frame. The Smith & Wesson .38 revolver, bottom, is stainless steel.

This old Colt 1903 is functionally sharp, but the original finish is mostly gone. If not well cared for it will rust quickly.

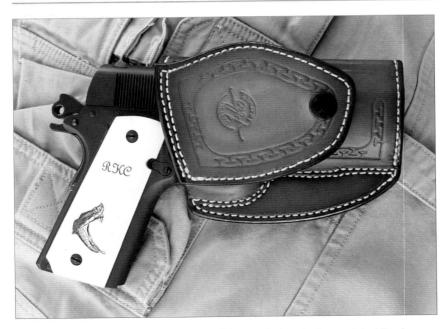

This matte blue Commander .45 is reasonably prepared against wear. It is riding in a Jeffrey Custom Leather holster. Note JMB distributing grip panels.

The forged-steel frame has a legitimate claim to being the strongest frame in the world, but the forging process is expensive. It isn't beating a handgun into shape over a blacksmith's anvil but rather by a power hammer. Steel blanks are forged into an approximation of the final form and then impacted with something on the order of one-hundred-pounds-per-square-inch pressure. Next comes heat treating and annealing. Milling, drilling, and tapping comes at some point. Forging and beating to shape and hammering into shape is an expensive process.

Casting is different. The casting process involves a wax mold that is molded as closely as possible to the desired dimensions of the final product. The wax mold is covered with a thin cast investment material that hardens and is resistant to heat. Casting is a mature technique that if done correctly produces a good product. Done cheaply, there may be bubbles or voids in the cast part. The mold is filled with molten metal. The wax mold melts and runs out of the investment shell. The casting hardens and the outer shell is broken away. Often the casting needs little finishing. Heat treating follows. If you think castings are weak, remember, Ruger uses castings, and its firearms are among the most respected hard-use firearms in the world. They get it right the first time. Modern CNC machinery offers fine dimensional control. Properly done casting is a reliable process.

Stainless steel is a bit more expensive to produce and machine than carbon steel. Stainless may be forged or cast. Don't be fooled by stainless-steel handguns. Stainless should be called stain/less, as it will rust and corrode and pit; it is simply far more difficult to convince stainless steel to begin to corrode. Aircraft-grade aluminum is strong and light and offers an alternative to steel for use in handgun frames. The primary advantage of aluminum is lightness; however, there are cautions concerning aluminum. As an example, the aluminum frame may be damaged more easily than a steel frame. This is borne out by my personal experience with several Colt Commander pistols over the years. In some cases the sharp nose of a semi-wadcutter bullet will take a nick out of the frame of the Commander. Once the anodizing is broken, wear proceeds quickly. This is another reason I never polish or throat a feed ramp. This type of damage sometimes leads to a new receiver, which is not inexpensive.

It is possible to damage the frame of an aluminum-frame automatic pistol by prying out steel parts. Care must be taken when dealing with aluminum-frame pistols. Some of the most durable handguns in the world use aluminum frames. These include the Colt Commander, the SIG P220, and the Beretta 92. Aluminum is a good material for handgun use. It is durable and will withstand many thousands of rounds of ammunition, but it will not stand as much abuse as a steel-frame pistol.

The newest material in general use is polymer. Polymer often contains plastic, and there are different types and grades of polymer. Polymer offers a lightweight inexpensive material that is easily cast and is resistant to oil and solvent. Polymer-framed pistols are often the winners of police competitions, not simply based on the merit of the particular handgun but because they are purchased on the low bid. An advantage of polymer is that when the pistol is fired the frame gives a little, which makes for more comfortable shooting. Blue-steel and walnut types will never accept polymer, but the material has a lot going for it. For hard use, polymer frames are more than acceptable.

HANDGUN FINISH

Steel in raw form rusts practically the moment it leaves the mill. It is highly desirable to provide some type of metal-finish protective coating to the handgun. Submersion in salts and in tanks of acid and other chemicals will stain or coat a metal with a protective finish. This is simply rust bluing. There is nothing more attractive than a deep blue finish, but bluing is not particularly durable. It is subject to wear and scratches.

Matte blue is less expensive to apply and more likely to wear quickly and corrode. Matte blue simply means the metal surface was not polished well before the pistol was blued. Matte blue is for all intents and purposes a less expensive and less durable blue finish. Various nickel finishes are beautiful when properly applied but not particularly durable. Nickel may chip and peel. I own a couple of Smith &

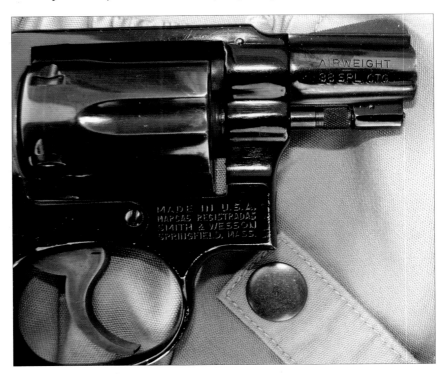

A subtle difference in the tone of the blue finish tells us that this Smith & Wesson features an aluminum frame. The cylinder and barrel are steel and blued; the frame is actually anodized.

Here is a modern handgun with a deep rich blue finish. Note the rubber ribber grips supplied with the Taurus Tracker.

Wesson revolvers with well done original nickel that have given decades of service, but I have seen quite a few poor aftermarket applications.

Nickel is applied by dipping the handgun in a tank filled with a chemical wash. A current is passed through the wash by means of an anode, resulting in the nickel adhering to the steel. A modern combination of electro-less nickel and Teflon comes from Robar Industries. This finish is applied without electrical current. NP3 is a space-age finish and a first-class addition to any working handgun. NP3 is highly resistant to wear and corrosion, and as a bonus NP3 is self-lubricating. NP3 is close to the ideal handgun finish. The same maker also offers Roguard, a darker finish with similar properties.

BearCoat is another Teflon-based finish that shows excellent lubricity. Self-lubricating and highly resistant to corrosion, BearCoat is nonreflective and available in several color schemes. I have used a number of BearCoat handguns over the past decade with excellent results. I have used BearCoat in blue, gray, and green. When it gets down to brass tacks, there is no substitute for proper maintenance, but a Teflon-based

This is a special custom pistol. The slide is Roguard, while the frame is NP3. This is a first-class carry gun for hard use.

This well worn old SIG is showing wear on the blued surface. The frame is aluminum and the Hogue grips are high-grade walnut.

finish is a great aid in keeping the handgun functioning and rust free. These modern finishes will add years to a handgun's life.

HANDGUN GRIP MATERIAL

When it comes to handgun grip material there are many choices, at least on the handguns that feature removable grip panels. Factory grips are often okay as issued, but there are many reasons for changing the grips. Pure pride of ownership and a degree of vanity are a legitimate reason. As an example, my personal stainless-steel Gold Cup .45 features a set of striking grips from JMB distributing. Tastefully done and with more than a little flair, these grips are longtime favorites.

A rather wild set of grips comes from CustomKillerGrips.com. These grips are made of rattlesnake skin. While there is a degree of in-your-face in these grips, the snake scales actually give good purchase. Hayes Holsters offers personalized handgun grips that reflect the spirit of the great artist who hand cuts each set of grips. Then we have Locrian grips, offering Thuya burl and other exotic woods at an affordable price.

While wood, and particularly the beautifully and durable cocobolo wood, is a good material for handgun grips, there are other materials that offer excellent adhesion when firing a serious combat handgun. Davidson Tool is among the makers offering first-class synthetic grips. These grips have plenty of adhesion, and they are quite rugged. Falco offers synthetic grips and has recently branched into wooden grips with a fresh perspective that gives them a unique product.

You have to decide which grips are best suited for your use. Is snag-free carry most important or will you be firing hundreds of rounds in competition? How much adhesion is needed? When all is said and done, the classic checkered grip from Smith and Alexander are first-class choices for any 1911 handgun.

Some of the high-production off-the-shelf makers offer good-quality grips. When it comes to taming the recoil of a heavy kicking handgun there is nothing quite like a Hogue MonoGrip. I have used the Hogue for many years with excellent results.

Perhaps the roughest and readiest of the modern autoloaders is the Glock. This long slide version features a Tennifer finish. *Glock Inc.*

Sometimes the Europeans get it right. This Astra Constable is almost forty years old, but the blue finish is still bright and shiny.

This is the author's high round count High Standard G Man. The grips are from Locrian and the finish is NP 3. This handgun is ready for another 20,000 rounds with no end in sight.

A close up of the NP 3 finish shows even coating. This is the recommended finish at present for hard use handguns.

While Hogue continues to offer tasteful choices in wooden grips when it comes to heavy kicking handguns, the MonoGrip is in a class by itself. When dealing with a snub .38 or similar compact revolver, the original Pachmayr Compac grips are ideal. I have fitted a set of these grips to my personal Airweight Model 12 .38 Special. Control remains good, and concealed carry is actually enhanced because the Compac grips are more compact than the factory wooden grips supplied with the Model 12.

Then there are the beautifully done, exquisite is a good word, stocks from Bear Hug. Perfectly mated to the hand and offering first-class checkering, these grips are simply the ne plus ultra of handgun grips. They are expensive but well worth both the price and the wait.

When all is said and done stainless steel is among the best materials for use with a hard-use pistol. This is the Beretta Tomcat, one of the few small automatic pistols the author trusts for reliability.

CHAPTER 17

Accessories

HOLSTERS FOR CARRY AND CONCEALMENT

IN TODAY'S WORLD THE PROSPECT of a deadly attack is a real possibility. I am not one of those who wishes to trade liberty for security. I realize that the presence of danger is a cost of liberty and one I am willing to bear. There are many places, forsaken of rational thought, that do not allow a permit to be issued at all, but most of the states have some form of shall issue law in place. It is not something to be taken lightly and neither is concealed carry for everyone. But it is a marker for liberty and justice.

Even if you are not certain you will find the concealed-carry lifestyle is for you, I recommend the process as educational for anyone who deems a handgun necessary for home defense. If you decide to carry a concealed handgun, you have to have something to carry the handgun in and we cannot resort to a bag or simply shove Old Ugly in the waistband. We need a good-quality load-bearing device that will not allow the handgun to shift, or worse, fall out of the pocket. A good-quality holster is a complement to the handgun. There are many styles and types. I do not expect everyone to

Of greatly different material, these are two very useful holsters. The Nemesis from DeSantis, left, and a first-class leather scabbard from Alessi, right.

Left to right, holsters from Alessi and Tauris, along with the COWS vest. It doesn't get any better than this.

order a one-at-a-time masterpiece from Hayes Holsters, but by the same token if you purchase a cheap holster it may break or fail at the worst moment. That Hayes holster looks pretty cheap in comparison to a funeral.

There are excellent choices in carry gear available from Alessi Holsters, Milt Sparks, Rhome DesBiens, and a few others. These are among the masters while up-and-coming makers such as Barber, Big River Leather, and Matthews are producing first-class carry gear. Then there are the utilitarian but well designed Kydex holsters from Fricke, Kolbeson, and NTAC. Do not despair is you are unable to lay down several hundred dollars for a custom rig. The workaday holsters from Falco are a reasonable investment in security.

When it comes to carry and concealment, some folks will tell you that you must have a small handgun. They fear a close inspection or perhaps a frisk. The fact is, you will seldom have this great a difficulty in concealing the handgun. There are environments in which discretion is absolutely necessary, but these situations are usually handled by carrying a snub-nosed .38 or a small-frame .45 automatic in an inside-the-waistband holster. I sometimes carry my personal (2.5-inch barrel) Smith & Wesson Model 19 .357 Magnum in a tuck-in holster from Active Pro. It is not completely comfortable; I know it is there, but the presence of such an effective handgun is comforting.

When we consider true concealed carry, the craft is practiced by many plain-clothes officers but also civilians. We are not obviously armed at first glance. We are undetected except by a pat down. Remaining undetected is vital. We remain discreet at all times. Few felons will attempt to attack a full-grown man unless they are armed. If he realizes you are armed beforehand, he may attack with a blow from behind, although he may defer and run. Discreet carry gives the armed citizen an element of surprise and an answer to the feral man's preemptive strike. If you are one of those who enjoys flashing the iron, then you need more help than I am able to give and you are headed for trouble.

Some carry a handgun with no holster, simply thrust in the belt. I suppose they are the type who go commando in other ways and avoid heavy lifting. A handgun thrust into the belt may slip at the worst moment. Sharp edges will abrade your skin. There are safety and practical issues to be avoided. The holster keeps the handgun in place for a rapid presentation and protects the body from sharp edges. Take a look at the strong side belt scabbard from Cotton Inks. This holster offsets the handgun from the body, affording a good draw angle. (This striking holster is also suitable for use as a showpiece or Bar B Q holster, but it is affordable.)

The handgun must remain secure during movement, and it is critical that it's always in the same place, properly presented for a rapid presentation. As an example, the well crafted Avenger-style holster from Ward Leather Company isn't as simply constructed as it first appears. The belt loop snuggle the holster close to the body, and expert boning makes for good security and speed. As the shooter makes the decision to draw or move to cover, he or she must be confident that the handgun is properly

A study in innovation: the Kolbeson IWB in Kydex with a lined component. Far right, the Haugen Handgun leather scabbard for a rail-light 1911.

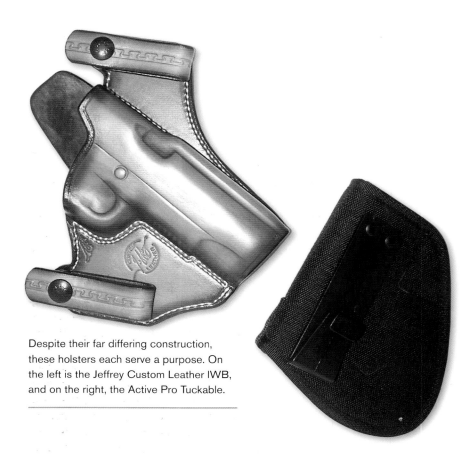

Despite their far differing construction, these holsters each serve a purpose. On the left is the Jeffrey Custom Leather IWB, and on the right, the Active Pro Tuckable.

holstered. A good holster and most of all a good-quality gun belt is essential. The gun belt must be of first quality leather capable of keeping the handgun and holster stable. A good-quality holster should be obtained along with a matching holster belt. I have been using the CC Leather convertible for some months with excellent results. While the alligator accent is quite arresting to the eye, the holster is secured to a good-quality Collins belt or it would not be efficient.

Some writers seem visited with acute oblivion and do not recognize the problems associated with concealed carry. Perhaps they have never carried a concealed handgun but only modeled the rigs in a studio. I think that two factors cause problems in concealed carry. One is choosing too large a gun and an inadequate holster and the other is choosing poor quality leather for the proper handgun. Some choose bad combinations all the way around. A good-quality holster such as the Secret Squirrel Practical is an immense aid in concealing a full-size pistol. The Secret Squirrel maker is a full-time law-enforcement professional who keeps a low profile and crafts first-class leather holsters. A full-size Glock may be too large and blocky for concealed carry, then the problem is compounded by choosing a cheap plastic belt slide holster.

I like the Government Model .45, which is considerably thinner than the Glock, and carry it in a quality piece of leather or horsehide. I prefer the strong side belt scabbard and sometimes carry the lighter Commander .45 or even a Defender .45, the light three-inch version of the 1911. I realize I am trading off effectiveness for convenience with the lighter handguns, but there simply must be a tradeoff in concealed carry. After all when we wear shorts and a T-shirt, concealed carry is more difficult.

The most popular holster is the strong side scabbard. The holster should be worn above the rear pocket and over the kidney region. The cylinder of the revolver should be carried above the belt to avoid the snake-swallowed-a-possum look. I have used truly excellent designs from Alessi. Although Lou Alessi has gone on, Alessi holsters survives and the craftsmen Lou trained are providing first-class leather with more than a little style. I own several original Alessi holsters from the 1980s, and the modern counterparts are at least comparable and in some cases indistinguishable from the original.

When you choose a good strong side scabbard be certain the pistol butt is angled into the body, which will result in good concealment under a light covering garment and the draw remains excellent. You don't belly up to the bar with a concealed-carry rig, but for most situations concealment is good. The fifteen-degree or FBI cant is ideal for concealed carry.

If you look closely at some of my holsters, you will note that they are double stitched and molded with attention to detail and blocking that ensures good fit and long life. As an example the BRL or Big River Leather holster is a study in how it is supposed to be done. The holster features a pinch in the trigger guard area for good retention and the holstering welt—in this case constructed from first-class alligator hide—is a great aid in retention and in reholstering. The holster isn't so light that it is unnoticed, but it will make carrying a heavy handgun bearable. The design is flawless.

INSIDE THE PANTS

By far the best choice for concealed carry when you must dress light is inside the waistband (IWB). The IWB holster is carried under the shirt and inside the pants. This allows the carrying of a serious concealed-carry handgun without the need for a long covering garment. Most of us will have some difficulty in acclimating to an IWB holster, but the time spent in getting used to the type is worthwhile. Among the better choices are those offered by US Gunleather. I have used a US Gunleather IWB with good results. The holster is light but offers good concealed carry.

From C5 Leather comes an IWB constructed of heavy-grade leather. This holster carries the handgun well, with good concealed carry, while maintaining an offset from the body. There are few if any designs better suited to concealed carry than the Milt Sparks Summer Special. This holster features a strong rein-forced holstering welt, a strong spine, excellent double stitching, and a sight track. This was the best engineered IWB ever when introduced, and even today, with

The are two Western-style holsters useful for anyone who needs top-grade gun leather. On the left is the Legends in Leather Justice, on the right, the Lobo Gun Leather Threepersons.

many competing designs, the Summer Special is the standard by which all others are judged.

For many years I have resisted the idea of a Kydex holster for concealed carry. Quite frankly I could not adapt to the material. Comfort was never a strong point of these holsters. The Kolbeson IWB has given me pause. This holster is actually comfortable and offers good concealment. While light, it is strong. But best of all the, Kolbeson design offers a lined option. This lining makes the holster fast, very fast. This is perhaps the fastest Kydex holster you will ever deploy. I am exploring Kydex at the moment and find the Kolbeson a front runner.

A first-class tactical rig for all around use is the Gideon from Dale Fricke. Fricke offers a number of Kydex concealed-carry designs that include a highly acclaimed appendix carry rig. These should be at the top of your list. NTAC is another maker of heavy-duty Kydex. I particularly like the versatility of the NTAC holsters as they are offered with interchangeable belt loops. They may be used as strong side holsters or inside the waistband holsters. This is real versatility.

PADDLE HOLSTERS

Paddle holsters are popular with those who have to remove and reholster the handgun often. Federal agents entering secure areas and those who often visit prisons and courtrooms either lock the piece in the vehicle or a locker. The paddle earns its name from the large ping-pong paddle-like attachment that slides into the pants. The holster is held only by friction. I do not like these holsters. For this type of duty I strongly prefer a holster with belt snaps that offers easy on-and-off holstering. The Milt Sparks Axiom is among the leading designs, and Carl Collins offers another.

Another alternative that many find appealing is the Jeffrey Custom Leather BTP (Better than a Paddle). The BTP is seen as an alternative to the paddle but also as an alternative for concealment for those who cannot tolerate an inside-the-waistband holster. The BTP slips under the belt and a flap with a belt snap goes over the belt and snaps in place. There is also a Kydex component that locks into the belt. This is a good kit that answers a real need.

The IWB answers a need for concealment. The crossdraw answers a need for access. If you are seated for most of the day or work in a vehicle, the crossdraw is the ideal choice. Care must be taken in choosing a crossdraw, as this is on the one holster type that absolutely must be done right. A poorly designed crossdraw is the poorest of holsters. The nuances of angle and design must be properly executed for comfort concealment and a good sharp draw. Crossdraw holsters are worn just toward the belt buckle away from the weak side hip. The holster should be snug and high riding against the body. The advantages of crossdraw carry are situational. If you are seated you may have your hand practically on the gun butt and access the handgun readily from this position. Currently, the front runner in crossdraw holsters is the Haugen Handgun Leather Huntington Wedge. This holster is well designed and constructed of good material.

These holsters are a study in exactly how it is done. The Alessi, left, is double stitched and features a holstering welt. This holster is over fifteen years old. The Axiom, right, is Milt Sparks' rendition of the belt-snap holster. They got it right.

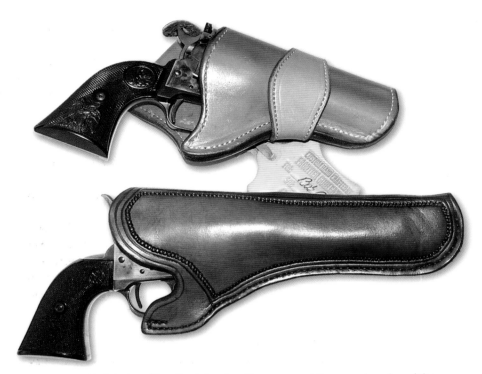

The Humboldt, left, from Bear Tooth Leather Company, and the crossdraw from John Bianchi's Frontier Gunleather, right, are among the author's favorite Western holsters. They are practical for field use.

SPACE AGE AND DUAL-PURPOSE

It would be nice to have one holster that fits more than one need. It is incredibly difficult to design a holster that does even one thing well, but we have a handful of holsters available that are true dual-purpose holsters. Among these are the combination holsters from NTAC. These holsters are supplied with standard belt loops that offer a good rigid carry in strong side use. They also are supplied with special belt clips that allow inside the trousers carry. I have often said we need two defensive pistols, the snub .38 and the 1911 .45. I have tested holsters from NTAC for each of these handguns. I give a resounding A+ to these holsters on every count.

SHOULDER HOLSTERS

Shoulder holsters are often uncomfortable and may even constrict breathing. Only the best made holsters are acceptable for constant carry. Modern shoulder holsters are more comfortable than ever and offer a wide range of adjustment. Today the concealed-carry shooter has knowledge once comprehensible only to experts. There are a few shoulder holsters that allow good comfortable carry and access as well. The shoulder holster must be anchored securely, and the holster cannot be boned too tightly to allow a good sharp draw. When testing a shoulder holster I begin by evaluating the security of the system. I holster the handgun in the holster with the holster off of the body. I vigorously shake the holster and determine if the handgun will break loose.

Among the most recent rigs to pass my comfort and security test is a holster from WestWoods Landing. This fabric holster had special hard plastic components and a geometrically designed harness that allows carrying the handgun comfortably for long periods of time. This rig keeps the handgun comfortable and also features two spare magazine carriers. This makes for a good balance of weight. I often carry my personal Beretta M9 in this rig. Not only is the WestWoods Landing shoulder holster comfortable, it gets the weight of the handgun off of the belt. This is a boon for those with injured or weak backs.

While I firmly believe that the gun load in the handgun should be used to solve the problem, it is nice to have a total of forty-five rounds of ammunition on tap when carrying this shoulder holster handgun and spare magazine combination.

The Lawman Leather Goods shoulder holster is among the classic designs well suited to concealed carry. This holster is the original Dirty Harry type. The Lawman Leather Goods holster is well made of good material. This is not an inexpensive holster, but it is a lifetime investment that offers good carry, comfort, and a sharp draw. If you have a real need to conceal a heavy handgun, this is a viable option. The strongly molded holster keeps the handgun secure, but the handgun may be drawn quickly by a practiced hand. This is good kit well worth your time and effort to master.

A lifetime investment in self-esteem comes from Hayes Leather. Note the laser-engraved personal motif and excellent tanning and stitching. The holster is also quite practical.

Three keepers from Cannon Leather, Cotton Inks, and John Bianchi's Frontier Gunleather: The Cotton Inks holster is extensively worked and personalized, the Cannon holster is a new design, and the Bianchi field holster is a classic design proven from forty years of production. Note differing levels of security, with a tab, an open top, and a thumb break, left to right.

These Kydex holsters from NTAC are completely versatile and ready for the most difficult duty. They get a clean bill of health on every count.

MORE ON CONCEALED-CARRY HOLSTERS

There are important differences in carry holsters. The strong side holster is the most important and serious thought should be given before you move away from this type of holster. Then there is the pancake, a design popularized by Roy Baker. The pancake lies flat against the body and allows good concealment under even a pulled-out T-shirt. The inside-the-waistband holster is the obvious first choice for deep concealment. The shoulder holster gets the weight of the handgun off of the belt and the crossdraw is the ideal choice for certain scenarios.

Among the top choices in pancake holsters is the Tribute, from Simply Rugged. This holster is designed as a tribute to Roy Baker and it makes the grade on every count. A rather nice hip-hugging pancake that I find true to the idea comes from Tucker Leather. I often carry this holster when deploying my Smith & Wesson Combat Magnum. Light, comfortable, and as flat as a revolver holster may be, this is a good choice for all-around concealed carry.

FIELD HOLSTERS

A good field holster is less complicated than a saddle harness but just about as important. Many saddle makers branched out into holster making, making good-quality leather holsters from skirting leather. One of these makers, El Paso Saddlery, is still with us today. It is interesting that many of the holsters designed

Two things the author could not do without: the RCBS registering trigger compression gauge and Wilson Combat ETM magazine.

for use by cowboys are still practical field holsters. They are comfortable holsters with a degree of security and they do the job.

Without the constraints of concealed carry these holster makers are free to produce a holster with comfort and security foremost in mind. We do not normally conceal the field holster, although from time to time it may be worn under the jacket to protect the handgun from moisture. (Always be aware of local laws.) When deer hunting, I sometimes carry my Springfield LW 1911 .45 as a backup to the rifle and to deal with coyote. I use a DeSantis shoulder holster, which is comfortable and sports a good draw angle.

As an aside in February 2009, a rabid coyote attacked a young girl at a school bus stop in South Carolina. Only rapid response by neighbors and the application of pistol fire stopped the attack. I like to have something with me in the field. When hunting in a headlong pursuit, such as boar hunting, a shoulder holster that keeps the handgun out of the way of brush and vines is a good choice. The significant difference when using a shoulder holster designed specifically for hunting is that the shoulder holster for field use may place a large heavy handgun more over the chest than under the arm.

Among the finest of all field holsters is the Diamond D custom holster by David Johnston. This holster was designed for Alaskan scouts. It had to be useful when carrying a backpack, for use over fishing waders, riding a four-wheeler, or when in a boat. The holster had to be adjustable so that it could be carried over a

coat if desired. The Guide's Choice features a retention screw and a hammer-reten-
tion device. Keeping the pistol secure is far more important than a fast draw. This
is among the single-most well-tested handgun holsters of all time. My personal
example is made up for the Ruger single-action revolver. A poorly fitted shoulder
holster is a chafing nuisance and not suited for field use. The Diamond D holster is
well suited for use in the wild.

A classic design worth your consideration is the Tom Threepersons holster.
Tom Threepersons was a lawman operating in the West just after World War I.
Threepersons took a Mexican Loop holster and cut it down until there was nothing
not needed and took it to S. D. Myres Saddlery. The rest is history. The classic
Threepersons is difficult for some to get right, but Lobo Gun Leather made my
example. I treasure this holster and often carry my vintage Smith & Wesson Model
27 with three-and-a-half-inch barrel in the Threepersons holster. Frankly, this is as
good as it gets and thanks to Lobo Gun Leather for keeping the design going.

A good modern design comes from Cannon Leather. Although there is no
safety strap, the design of the holster keeps the revolver secure with a molded tap.
This is a good-looking holster that offers excellent fit, finish, and style. Cannon is a
relatively new maker but one with much promise.

This is the Guide's Choice holster. While few of us will hunt in the harsh conditions of
Alaska, the holster was designed for it and is arguably the best of the breed.

Personal-defense handgun holsters carry the handgun in the proper position for a fast draw but they are often designed to ride close to the body for concealed carry and this may not be ideal when wearing hunting togs. Among the best field holsters I have used for Magnum revolvers is the Frontier Gunleather 275 Liberty Quicksnap. This holster features a well designed retention snap, and the angle of the holster offsets the handgun from the body for a good draw. If you carry a revolver in uniform, as many park rangers do, this is a good design. I prefer this holster for outdoors carry with the Smith & Wesson Model 25 .45 Colt.

I mentioned I often carry my outdoors handguns in cowboy-style holsters. I simply like the look and the Western styling. The Western Star line is particularly attractive. There is something attractive about carrying a Colt 1911 .45 in a field holster designed prior to World War I, but Western Star and maker John Costanza are at the top of my list for pure show and style.

Another great holster for all around use is the Humboldt by noted maker Ralph Hunt Williams. Williams operates Bear Tooth Leather Company. Williams has taken cowboy leather to the top of his class with his River Series, named for great rivers of the West. I have examined quite a few original holsters from the Western era, and with all respect due, I have never seen an original of the quality produced by Williams. Modern makers simply produce first-class gear for discerning shooters.

Flap holsters are overlooked but still serve well for field use. The original flap holster was designed to protect the powder charge and caps of black powder revolvers from moisture and rough handling. I have used a quality reproduction holster from the Australian company Percival often when packing my Dixie Gun Works .44-caliber cap-and-ball revolver. I enjoy this revolver very much and when roughing it, why, this is a great revolver.

You cannot be tactical at all times, and here I am parting company with some of my peers in the tactical community. I do not feel that I am taking my life in my hands by hiking with a black powder revolver rather than a model Magnum. There is the balance and heft on the hip nothing else has. The revolver is light enough, but anyone who does not respect the .457-inch ball thrown by this revolver is foolish. Keeping in touch with history is important and leather makers such as Bianchi, Constanza, Percival, and Williams keep the Old West alive.

While the caps were once the main area of concern, today the finish of the handgun is protected by flap holsters. I have seen handguns corroded by blood from game as the hunter packs the meat out, and a good flap holster, such as the ones offered by Triple K, protect the handgun. I have used a nice custom flap holster from Our Bandit Leather Crafters with excellent results. This one is molded for the Ruger .22, a good squirrel gun.

WHERE DO I FIND IT?

I receive enquiries often from concealed-carry permit holders who cannot find the holster they need. A bit of research usually turns up the right combination.

As an example, I have recently adopted a light rail pistol for professional use. The Springfield LW Operator is a first-class all-around modern handgun. I was not exactly led kicking and screaming into the modern era. I like this handgun very much, but holstering the piece wasn't easy. Fortunately, prior experience and my extensive contacts led to Secret Squirrel Leather and Haugen Handgun Leather.

Why do I turn to working cops and former cops for my leather? Like retired chief Roy Cory at Lobo Gun Leather, it is because they know what the hell they are doing. Secret Squirrel supplied an IWB holster with an adjustable belt loop for a rail gun, and Jerry Evans at Haugen produced a great belt scabbard that is among the fastest designs I have ever used for the rail gun. They are good enough for who they are for.

SPECIAL MENTION

Among the great names in leather is Jim Lockwood who runs Legends in Leather. He appreciates the rich heritage of American gun leather. Some of the rigs illustrated in the chapter on single-action revolvers are his. The illustrations speak for themselves. Lockwood also offers a concealed-carry holster that is unique in many ways. This holster is comfortable, concealable, and offers a true fast-draw angle. This is an expensive holster, but well worth the price. The example illustrated was worn for months by Lockwood as he perfected the design. If the production Justice is even better than this one, Lockwood has outdone himself. His work is a piece of Americana, and every one of his rigs is well worth their price.

OTHER ACCESSORIES

The traditional concealed-carry vest is done in many ways. Among my favorites are those from Concealed Carry Outfitters. These vests feature built-in holsters and have plenty of secure pockets. I still prefer carrying my handgun in a holster, but as you grow older and more experienced you realize the more gear the better. The pockets of these vests carry lights, knives, notebooks, and other necessary items. I admit to occasionally stashing a backup snub .38 in these voluminous pockets. After all, a snub .38 may be fired through a pocket if necessary. I also use these vests in the great outdoors. They are great for carrying water bottles and other gear.

COWS VEST

The Classic Old West Styles vest is heavier than most and well suited to carry during the winter months. While there are other lightweight and heavy vests this one strikes my fancy. It is Western in styling but at home in any environment. My son the military intelligence officer has borrowed mine for "evaluation" so I may never see it again. It is that good.

EOTAC

EOTAC ads ask you to become the "gray man," to become invisible with your weapons well concealed. I agree. EOTAC jeans and shirts are comfortable, long wearing, and first class in every way. Unlike some types, they do not look odd or scream "pistol." These are well designed garments worth your attention.

LIFE-SAVING ACCESSORIES

A pistol magazine isn't an accessory but a vital part of the handgun; however, the magazine wears and must be replaced from time to time. For the majority of my pistols I use magazines from the maker. SIG for SIG, Beretta in the Beretta. There are exceptions. The Wilson Combat ETM magazine is a modern magazine for the 1911 pistol. The Metalform magazines are a favorite of professionals and virtually the only choice in 10mm and .38 Super 1911 pistols. I have used Novak magazines for the 1911 with excellent results. Recently I became aware of Novak magazines for the SIG P220. After some test and evaluation I traded out all of my SIG P220 magazines for the Novak product. These are good magazines well worth their price.

CHAPTER 18

Ammunition and Handloading

WHEN YOU LOOK AT AMMUNITION you must decide what job you will put the load to. What is the criteria? Is ballistic performance most important or is accuracy essential? Is the load and gun combination required to group five shots into two inches at fifteen yards or fifty yards? Do you need a hollow point or is an inexpensive lead bullet just fine? Does safety demand a sintered bullet?

The bottom line is most users purchase ammunition without considering the mission. There are loads that maximize every caliber, but until the laws of physics are changed a larger bullet lets out more blood and lets more air in. You cannot circumvent these rules. Some of the changes made to handgun bullets are merely cosmetic. The energy of a cartridge and its ability to do damage may be changed by stepping up the powder charge and using exotic bullet styles, but large calibers are always more effective given comparable loadings.

The calibers that benefit the greatest from the use of hollow point bullets are the medium calibers, the 9mm, .38 Special, and .357 Magnum. The big bores do not need help as badly. The lighter calibers suffer from limited penetration as it is, and a hollow-point bullet may further limit this penetration. The single most important quality a defensive or hunting bullet must possess is penetration. The bullet must have sufficient

If you need top-notch accuracy and good performance then Black Hills ammunition will deliver.

Speer Gold Dot loads are great performers. These were fired at different velocities in a .357 Magnum revolver. Good performance begins at 1,200 feet per second with the 158-grain bullet.

Left to right: the PowRBall, 110-grain JHP, and DX load, all .38 Special, all first class from Cor Bon.

penetration to reach the organs. With sufficient penetration ensured by an adequate caliber, we may look to improving the wound potential by deploying an expanding bullet. There isn't an arcane science such as alchemy at work. Beware of ridiculous claims. Look for solid performance.

The reputable ammunition companies have invested millions in product development. Competition is fierce. The primary differences in expanding bullet loads are the balance of penetration and expansion. Some penetrate deeper than others; others expand more and penetrate less. Look to quality and cartridge integrity as your baseline.

I think that it is well worth your time to study handloading. While handloading or reloading is not for everyone, if you wish to master the handgun, then the amount of ammunition demanded requires that you handload. The reason that handloaders are able to produce such economical ammunition is simple. Handloaders reuse the most expensive part of ammunition time and time again. The brass cartridge case is a renewable resource.

I strongly advise you to purchase a good reloading manual and a volume that gives the details of handloading. In a nutshell, handloading involves recycling the spent cartridge case. In a series of operations using a die press and various dies, including sizing dies and seating dies, the handloader resizes a spent cartridge case and in the process decaps the spent primer. A new primer (cap) is inserted into the cartridge case and the case mouth is flared slightly to accept a pistol bullet. The case is charged with the appropriate powder charge, and then a bullet is seated in the case. The final step is crimping the bullet in place.

Quite a few of us enjoy handloading for its own sake. If you are not responsible and cannot follow directions do not attempt handloading. This is no place for reck-lessness or inattention to detail, but for many of us reloading allows good economy, the ability to produce tack-driving accurate loads, and even the opportunity to improve the performance of a caliber.

The author uses primarily handloads for practice. Oregon Trail, WW 231, and Starline brass is a good combination.

PRACTICE LOADS

The subject of practice loads is a simple one for me. I simply use good hard cast bullets at moderate velocity in all my handguns. This means handloads. When addressing loading lead bullets, first begin with a clean bore. If the handgun barrel is rough then the pits or tool marks will seriously affect handgun accuracy. The handgun will lead badly. Copper jackets also leave deposits, and firing lead over copper deposits adversely affects accuracy.

Use a copper brush and then a clean patch and be certain your bore is kept clean for maximum accuracy. A lead bullet must be close to bore diameter for a good gas seal. The chamber of cylinder throat is larger than the rifling and allows gas to escape to some extent or the other, but once the bullet hits the rifling there should be good fit. Good tight revolvers such as the USFA Rodeo and the Smith & Wesson revolver usually offer good fit and accuracy, but less expensive revolvers may be problematic. Even Smith has occasionally experienced problems with the throat from time to time.

Hot gas will sometimes melt the lube from the bullet if excess blowby is present. This means we have unlubricated lead in the bore, which is never a good thing. It is true that bullets slug up in the bore to an extent, but if you like low-velocity practice loads there isn't a lot of slugging up. There are no real drawbacks with lead bullets, simply trade-offs. You may ask yourself how many rounds you are going to fire this year. If you are planning on firing more than a few hundred then you need to be handloading or get ready to max out the platinum credit card.

Lead is easy on the barrel and may exhibit stellar accuracy. During the past ten years I have strived for consistent and economical results in handloaded ammunition. I have looked for the tugboat, for reliable and hard working ammunition. Others have pursued the overloaded ferry and the excitement of a too heavy load that occasionally gives a fantastic blow up. I look for interesting things of which to bear witness, but blowing up a handgun is not one of them. I download my personal practice loads. As an example, the standard 230-grain FMJ .45 ACP

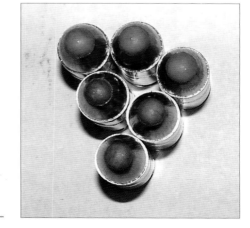

These are Glaser Safety Slugs. They are formidable carry loads, limiting penetration and ensuring tissue disruption.

factory load clocks about 820 feet per second. I normally load the Oregon Trail 230-grain RNL bullet at 780 to 790 feet per second for practice. I test many .45s and low recoil and modest cost are highly desirable. So is accuracy.

Let me explain a few differences between lead and jacketed bullets. You will note that lead bullets are delivered in larger diameter than jacketed bullets. A .44-caliber jacketed bullet will run .429 ,while the lead bullet will make .430 or even .431. This is simply to be certain the bore is sealed and that the bullet takes the grooves. When I use jacketed bullets I use those that are noted either for excellent expansion or for top-notch accuracy. The Nosler 185-grain JHP is among the best match-grade bullets in .45 ACP. The 200-grain Speer Gold Dot is a particular favorite because it opens at modest velocity and retains the majority of its bullet weight. The Hornady XTP bullet offers excellent accuracy and good penetration. There are many applications for these jacketed bullets.

When it comes to swaged bullets I defer from using them. These are soft lead bullets pressed into shape. I do not care for these bullets because they are too soft and often produce excess leading at velocities over 850 feet per second. The bullets are often accurate but too expensive compared to lead bullets. The simplest bullets are best. A round-nose cast bullet is well suited to automatic pistols because it feeds well.

This is a Glaser Safety Slug after impacting a water jug. I find this impressive.

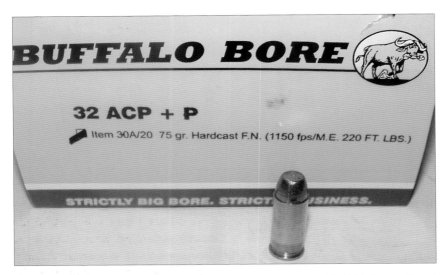

The Buffalo Bore loads maximize each caliber, even the little .32 ACP. This is a preferred load if you deploy the mouse gun.

In revolvers, the SWC is popular and usually very accurate. The SWC is a good choice because of its blunt nose. This blunt nose is a great killer on large game and also a good choice for small game. Lead offers less resistance in the bore than jacketed bullets and may produce higher velocity with the same powder charge. Inexpensive lead bullet loads are the key to affordable practice and improving the accuracy potential of any handgun.

If you are not a handloader, then remanufactured loads are a good resource. Black Hills ammunition offers the Blue Box remanufactured line. They work just great. Black Hills purchases spent brass in order to offer these loads. Other companies work differently; you send them your brass to be reloaded. MasterCast is among these. I have enjoyed excellent luck with MasterCast over the past decade. There are always resources other than premium factory loads for practice. Save your brass and you will be ahead of the game.

SINTERED LOADS

SinterFire is the leader in frangible technology. Simply put, the bullet is a type of dust glued together. When the bullet strikes a steel target it disintegrates. I have enjoyed excellent results with these bullets in training. They make for added safety in shooting steel targets. They are available as factory loads and as a component for handloading.

MATCH-GRADE LOADS

Also called target loads, match-grade loads are held to a high standard of accuracy. The handloader will be certain that each case holds, as precisely as is possible, the same powder charge. He will use a proven match-grade bullet such as the Nosler 185-grain JHP. For those who use factory ammunition in bull's-eye matches, Federal Match is legendary. An up-and-coming load with good performance is the Cor Bon Performance Match. For the shooter who demands the best, these loads perform to Match standards. They are not cheap, but they get the job done.

This is the Winchester .38 Special FBI load. It doesn't get better.

WORKING LOADS

A conservative amount of research results in finding a good reliable load for all-around use. This includes target practice to the longest practical handgun range and taking game as well. A standard bullet weight (160 grains in the .357 Magnum and 230 grains in the .45 ACP, 240 grains in the .44 Magnum) works well with a moderate powder charge. The .45 Colt is a more difficult cartridge to use because it was designed to be filled with black powder. Just the same, a .45 Colt 255-grain SWC has a frontal diameter of 1.6 inches. This is a lot of bullet. I have used Unique powder in loading this cartridge and continue to do so. At 1,000 feet per second this big bullet is something to contend with. While blowby is sometimes a problem, the .45 Colt can be mastered.

HUNTING LOADS

When we first look at hunting loads, we may wonder if any handgun caliber is appropriate for hunting game with a handgun. After all a .30-06 rifle produces some 2,500 foot-pounds of energy with standard loads. The .44 Magnum revolver produces 1,000 foot-pounds at its best. But equal amounts of energy is not the whole picture. A full-power .44 Magnum load with a properly designed bullet has plenty of penetration, and penetration is what counts. As a bonus, the bullet that is penetrating so deeply has a frontal diameter of 1.5 inch. That adds up to a lot of damage.

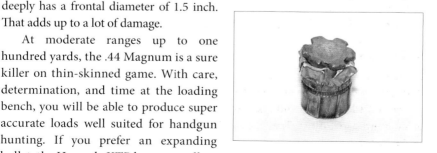

At moderate ranges up to one hundred yards, the .44 Magnum is a sure killer on thin-skinned game. With care, determination, and time at the loading bench, you will be able to produce super accurate loads well suited for handgun hunting. If you prefer an expanding bullet, the Hornady XTP has an excellent reputation for accuracy, penetration, and expansion. The balance of expansion and penetration is ideal for hunting. Another

This is typical Hornday XTP expansion, consistent and with the expanded stellate nose.

good choice is the Barnes all-copper bullet. As reports come in from the field, this bullet is earning a good reputation. When working with hunting handloads the powder charge must be consistent. I often weigh each charge individually to produce the top accuracy. Naturally the factory cannot do this and my handloads are more accurate than all but the most exceptional factory loads.

PERSONAL-DEFENSE LOADS

The subject of personal-defense ammunition is important. When you make a wrong choice the inadequacies of the load may resound later. In interviewing those who have survived gunfights, with inverse questions concerning the aberrant rather than the routine, I have reached definite conclusions concerning personal-defense ammunition. Let's yank the thread in your brain and start thinking. Only your soul knows your capacity for combat, but we know what criminals are capable of.

Some may think I love the .45 in the way an indulgent man loves his incorrigible self-indulgent wife, but that is not the case. The big-bore handguns work and they are proven. This is forthright news and street savvy if you will. If you deploy a small bore, then you have to do your best to encourage the small bore to act like a big bore. You will fool some of the people some of the time with this trick using expanding bullets and being fairly well armed.

All factory ammunition is not created equal. You will not find the bargain-basement ammunition covered in this chapter. I have fired them and you should too. Shoot the stuff and you will realize it isn't as accurate or clean burning as Black Hills, Cor Bon, Federal, Fiocchi, Hornady, or Winchester. Reliability is the first criteria. The load should always feed. This is cycle reliability. The bullet nose must also feed up the feed ramp. This is feed reliability. I test ammunition for resistance to oil, solvent, and water. I make certain that the bullet nose is not pressed into the cartridge case, even if we chamber the same cartridge several times.

Once reliability and accuracy are established we look to ballistic effect on the target. Adequate penetration is essential. If the felon is wearing heavy clothing, the bullet must penetrate through this clothing and to the vital organs. If the felon is firing at you with his arms outstretched, then the bullet may have to penetrate through these heavy bones and reach the vital organs. Nothing is guaranteed, and a hollow-point bullet may expand or it may not, but if it reaches the organs and cuts a hole the chances are the effect will be what we are looking for. Some criminals are big men with hardened muscles. A frangible bullet may under penetrate. There are excellent choices in every caliber.

The problem with recommending a specific load is that the ammunition picture changes often. I do not wish this book to become a dated reference. The requirements for personal-defense loads are constant, but there are new loads with new technology—or so they claim—introduced regularly. As long as the criteria for a personal-defense load is maintained, these loads are acceptable and may indeed offer the edge they claim. The personal-defense loading should penetrate twelve

Let accuracy be your guide. If the shooter tightens up these groups, fired at twenty-five yards, it should be within three inches.

These are cast bullet loads in the little .32 Smith & Wesson Long, using the Magnus 100-grain hard-cast SWC bullet. This is a fine small-game load.

This is the 158-grain XTP fired with the Black Hills .357 Magnum load. Good performance and great accuracy.

inches in a ballistic media that is designed to approximate a human target. I use the *Gun Tests* magazine criteria. I shoot galloon water jugs. They measure six inches across the widest point. If the bullet stops in the far side, expanded, it has reached twelve inches. This is a simplistic criteria and ballistic gelatin behaves differently, but this is a test program that all of us are able to do on our own time and with our own dime.

When you look at ammunition there is a lot of information. It isn't all hype. Hype doesn't shoot well like the Cor Bon Performance Match, and hype doesn't expand like the Black Hills TAC load. But take your own counsel. Fire a lot of ammunition, and look for good powder burn and accuracy. I hope you take my words to heart, but in the end it is your hide.

Appendix
Ammunition Loads

Below are a few representative loads I have worked up for my personal Ruger Super Blackhawk. I have included Cor Bon hunting loads as a comparison. Cor Bon is a semi-custom operation that produces match-grade accurate hunting loads.

.44 Magnum Hunting Loads
Fired from 7.5-inch Ruger Super Blackhawk

Hornady 240-grain XTP	25.0 H110	1,315 fps
Nosler 240-grain JHP	20.5 VV N110	1,340 fps
Speer 270-grain Gold Dot	16.5 VV N110	1,160 fps
Hornady 300-grain XTP	20.4 H 110	1,222 fps

Cor Bon factory .44 Magnum Loads

180-grain JHP	1,680 fps
240-grain JHP	1,475 fps
260-grain JSP	1,350 fps
300-grain JSP	1,259 fps
320-grain Penetrator	1,175 fps

You will find that the claims of some companies are hollow. Their bullets may only expand if they hit a brick wall. Others over penetrate with little expansion. A few under penetrate. I have gone out on a limb and listed some of the better loads in each caliber, circa 2011. It will be interesting to see what the future holds, but currently, these are among the better choices.

.38 Special

Black Hills 125-grain JHP	Heavy on penetration. Very accurate.
Buffalo Bore 125-grain JHP	Accurate, good expansion
Buffalo Bore 158-grain LSWCHP	Long on penetration, heavy recoil
Cor Bon 110-grain DXP	Accurate, good penetration
Cor Bon 110-grain JHP	Good expansion
Speer 135-grain JHP +P	A highly developed load specifically for snub-nose revolvers
Winchester 158-grain SWC HP	A classic .38, once used by the .FBI and never a bad choice

9mm Luger

Black Hills 115-grain EXP	A non-+P load, easy to control, with good expansion.
Black Hills 115-grain +P	Among the most impressive 9mm loads, accurate, with good expansion and penetration; a good service load.

9mm Luger

Black Hills TAC	Using the 115-grain Barnes bullet, this load displays all of the advantages of the solid copper bullet
Cor Bon 115-grain JHP	This load is often among the fastest factory loads in this weight class. The Cor Bon load fragments and penetrates to the minimum acceptable amount, which is useful in an urban load.
Cor Bon 115-grain DPX	Using the space age Barnes X bullet, this load offers good penetration and expansion.
Fiocchi 115-grain XTP	Faster than most in this class and using the Hornady XTP bullet, this is a high-quality load that is often quite accurate.
Speer 124-grain Gold Dot +P	This is a popular service load with a generally good track record for the caliber.
Winchester 124-grain Talon +P	This load is a good example of modern technology and excellent penetration.

.357 Magnum

Cor Bon 110-grain JHP	Easily controlled and offering fragmenting performance, this is a good urban load.
Federal 130-grain Hydra Shock	This load exits my four-inch barrel .357 Magnum at a blistering 1,480 fps. For those who are able to control the Magnum, this is superb performance, with wild expansion and fragmentation.
Winchester 110-grain JHP	A fragmenting load that is loaded to about 1,300 fps from a four-inch barrel, making it easy to control in double-action pairs.
Winchester 145-grain Silvertip	A strong load with an excellent balance of expansion and penetration.

.357 SIG

Cor Bon 115-grain JHP	Hot and fast!
Speer 125-grain JHP Gold Dot	A good all-around service load
Hornady 124-grain XTP	Per my test program, this load offers the single best penetration against vehicle sheet metal of any police type loading in any caliber. (Published in *Police Magazine*.)

.357 SIG

Winchester 125-grain Silvertip	The classic Super load
Cor Bon 125-grain JHP	The one load that maximizes the Super

.40 Smith & Wesson

Black Hills 155-grain TAC	This is another top-flight load from Black Hills using the TAC Bullet.
Black Hills 165-grain JHP	With an excellent potential for penetration and retained weight, this is an ideal all-around service load.
Cor Bon 135-grain JHP	This is generally agreed upon as the most dynamic expanding of all .40 loads.
Cor Bon 150-grain JHP	Among the most accurate .40 loads, it's nearly as dynamic as the 135-grain load but with better accuracy.
Speer 155-grain Gold Dot	This has a good serviceable all-around loading for the .40.
Winchester 155-grain Silvertip	This is the classic Silvertip expansion.

10mm

Hornady 155-grain XTP	An excellent all around choice in this hard hitting caliber
Cor Bon 135-grain JHP	A good urban load

.45 ACP

Black Hills 185-grain TAC	This is a first-class all-around service and defense load using the Barnes all copper bullet.
Cor Bon 200-grain JHP	This is a good fast-expanding load that delivers good accuracy.
Black Hills 230-grain JHP	This is a good service load with all around good performance.
Cor Bon 230-grain JHP +P	If you need more power than the standard .45 ACP, this is the choice.
Speer 230-grain Gold Dot	A relatively mild load, easy to control, and brilliantly accurate, it performs well even in short-barrel handguns.
Winchester 230-grain Bonded Core	This is the choice of the FBI.

Index

Alessi, Lou, 223
ammunition, 235–249
    hunting loads, 241–242
    match-grade loads, 240–241
    personal defense loads, 242–243
    practice loads, 238–240
    sintered loads, 240
    working loads, 241
automatic, 59–71, 102–111
    1911, 120, 221, 234
    Action Works .45, 160
    Armalite AR 24, 61
    Astra Constable, 201, 215a
    Beretta, 161, 200–201
      2, 61
      53, 92, 191, 193, 199, 206, 211
      60, 63, 68–69, 92–93, 102–104, 160, 162
      1934, 55
      1951, 55
      Cougar, 63, 162
      M 9, 102, 105, 110, 162, 179, 193, 199, 203, 227
      Model 21A, 154
      Tomcat, 217
    Bersa, 201
    Bren Ten, 60
    Browning, 110
      Buckmark, 63–64
      High Power, 64, 105
    Colt, 110
      1911, 52–53, 55, 60–62, 66, 105–106, 142, 155, 194, 206–207, 232
      Commander .45, 223
      Gold Cup, 158

      National Match, 158
      Targetsman, 103
      Woodsman .22, 154
    cycle reliability, 108–111
    CZ
      52, 60
      60–61, 67, 75, 99, 107, 207
    Defender .45, 223
    EAA Witness, 61
    feed, 108–111
    Glock, 62, 65, 68, 108, 148, 194, 200, 215, 222
      Model 17, 63, 68, 142
      Model 19, 63
      Model 20, 66, 91–92
      Model 21, 88, 92
      Model 36, 194
      Model 37, 101
    Government Model .45, 223
    Heckler & Koch
      P7M8, 61, 64, 105–106
      Universal Service Pistol, 61, 63, 66
    High Standard G Man, 216
    Kimber
      .45, 105
      1911, 107, 194
      CDP, 194
      Custom II, 71
      Custom Defense Pistol, 71
      Gold Combat, 71, 194
      Gold Target, 71
    Les Baer, 201
      1911, 194
    Luger, 106, 110, 200, 246
    Makarov, 110

Mauser, 105, 148
   C 96, 106
Ruger, 69–70
   .22/.45, 143
   345, 69
   Magnum, 170
   P89, 69
   P90, 69
   P94, 70
   SR 17, 70
   Standard Model, 63
   Super Blackhawk, 170, 172
SIG SAUER, 105, 121, 142, 162, 200,
   203, 214
   .357, 247–248
   P220, 61–62, 66, 68, 93, 107
   P225, 61
   P226, 61, 68
   P228, 61
   P229, 61, 67–68
   P250, 108
Smith & Wesson
   .40, 248
   .45, 209
   Combat Magnum, 229
   Magnum, 170
   Military and Police (M&P), 68,
   69, 194
   Model 19, 220
   Model 25 .45 Colt, 232
   Model 39, 59
   Model 59, 59
Springfield
   1911, 194
   LW 1911, 230
   LW Operator, 194
   Professional, 70
   XD, 71, 106
Taurus, 68–70
   24/7, 69, 142
   809, 65
   Magnum, 170
   PT 92, 69
Walther PPK, 201
Wilson Combat 1911, 194
Applegate, Col. Rex, 186
Baker, Roy, 229
Beretta, 191
Bianchi, John, 228
Black Hills, 24
Borchardt, Hugo, 47
Browning, John Moses, 47, 50, 93, 95

Browning, 191
Cash, Johnny, 31
Cody, Buffalo Bill, 12
Colt, Samuel, 21, 23, 93
Colt Firearms, 95, 191
Cooper, Col. Jeff, 60, 165
Costanza, John, 23, 232
CZ, 191
Davis, Sammy Jr., 31
defense, personal, 180–181
Dixie Gunworks, 10
Earp, Wyatt, 14
Fabrique Nationale, 95
Feedrele, Fidel, 48
Feedrele, Freidrick, 48
Feedrele, Josef, 48
finish, 212–214
Fiocchi, 48–49
garments, EOTAC, 234
Glock, 191–192
Graff, Jenny, 137–138
grip material, 214–217
holster, 219–233
   Active Pro, 220
      Tuckable, 222
   Alessi, 186, 219–220, 223, 225
   Bar B Q, 221
   Barber, 220
   Bear Tooth Leather Company, 226, 232
   Big River Leather (BRL), 206, 220, 223
   C5 Leather, 223
   Cannon Leather, 170, 228, 231
   Carl Collins (CC), 225
      Leather, 222
   concealed-carry, 229
   Cotton Inks, 221, 228
   cowboy, 232
   crossdraw, 225
   Dale Fricke Gideon, 224
   David Johnston Diamond D, 230–231
   DeSantis
      IWB, 93
      Nemesis, 219
      shoulder, 230
   dual-purpose, 226
   El Paso Saddlery, 229
   field, 229–232
   flap, 232
   Fricke, 220
   Frontier Gunleather, 228
      274 Liberty Quicksnap, 232
      crossdraw, 226

GDS, 148
Guide's Choice, 231
Haugen Handgun Leather, 162, 221,
    225, 233
  Huntington Wedge, 225
Hayes, 220
  Leather, 227
Humboldt, 232
inside the waistband (IWB), 223–225
Jeffrey Custom Leather, 40, 210
  Leather BTP, 225
  Leather IWB, 222
Justice, 233
Kolbeson, 220, 221, 224
  Kolbeson IWB, 224
Kydex, 220–221, 224–225, 229
Lawman Leather Goods, 227
Legends in Leather, 21, 233
  Justice, 224
Lobo Gun Leather, 231, 233
  Threepersons, 172, 224
Matthews, 220
Mexican Loop, 231
Milt Sparks, 220
  Axiom, 225
  Summer Special, 223–224
NTAC, 220, 224, 226, 229
Null shell, 107
Our Bandit Leather Crafters, 232
paddle, 224–226
Percival, 9, 25, 232
pistol, 85
Ranger, 94
Rhone DesBiens, 220
S. D. Myres Saddlery, 231
Secret Squirrel
  Leather, 233
  Practical, 222
shoulder, 82, 226–227
Simply Rugged Tribute, 229
Tauris, 220
Threepersons, 95, 231
Triple K, 232
Tucker
  Leather, 229
  pancake, 141
US Gunleather, 223
Ward Leather Company, 221
Western, 158, 224
  Star Leather, 23
WestWoods Landing, 227
handfit, 141–143

Heckler & Koch, 191
Hickock, Wild Bill, 30
hunting
  aim, 178
  game size, 177–178
  kill zones, 175–177
  Magnum calibers, 178
Interarms, 47
International Defense Pistol Association
    (IDPA), 160–165, 181, 184
International Practical Shooting
    Competition (IPSC), 165
John Inglis, 51
Jordan, Paul, 73
Kimber, 62, 191
King, D. W., 77
King, Walter, 77
Lawrence, T. E., 15, 23
Lockwood, Jim, 21, 233
Luger, Georg, 47
Lund, Erik, 164
MacArthur, Douglas, 30
maintenance
  automatics, 200
  finish, 207–208
  lubrication, 204, 206
  springs, 206–207
marksmanship
  aim, 126–127
  breath control, 128–129
  calling the shot, 131, 134
  dry fire, 133–134
  eye dominance, 124
  firing with one hand, 125–126
  follow-through, 131
  grip, 124–125
  off-hand shooting, 132
  rest, 129
  shooting a target, 134
  shots, low, 134
  trigger control, 133
  triggernometry, 129–131
material, metal, 75–77
Mauser, Paul, 47
Maxim, Hiram, 47
Munden, Bob, 166–167
Navy Arms, 11
New York City Police Department, 44
pistol
  .357 Magnum, 247
  .44 Magnum, 245
  Airweight Model 12, 216

Argentine High Power, 55
Astra, 117
Bersa .22, 154
Borchardt, 47
Browning, 50–51, 117
    Astra, 51
    Buckmark, 139
    High Power, 51–55
Colt
    1900, 95
    1903, 56–57, 210
    Commander, 206, 210–211
    Gold Cup, 45, 85, 160, 214
    Officers Model Match, 158
    Official Police, 154
Combat Masterpiece, 116
CZ P 01, 205
Glock, 202, 206
Heckler & Koch, 129, 140, 186
    P7, 52, 55
    P30, 195
    USP, 195
High Standard Double Nine, 153
Hornady XTP, 177
Kimber Eclipse, 92
Les Baer, 160
Long 7.56mm, 54
Luger, 48, 54, 60
    .30, 48–50, 52, 123
MAC 50, 55
MAS 35, 52
magazine, 234
Mauser
    C 96, 48–49, 51, 53
    HSc, 47
    M 96, 47
    Red 9, 49
Nambu, 55
pocket, 56–57
Radom, 49, 53
    ViS wz.35, 52–53
Ruger, 135
    .22, 232
    .22/45, 140
    Hunter, 150
    P89, 140
    Standard Model, 136, 139,
        153–154, 160
    Super Blackhawk, 167, 245
Savage 1910, 56
self-loading, 47–57

SIG SAUER
    Mosquito, 139
    P220, 91, 130, 192–193, 211, 234
    P226, 191
    P229, 193
    P250, 193
Smith & Wesson
    double-action .22, 154
    K 38, 62, 158
    Military and Police (M&P), 148
    Model 27, 231
    Model 39, 56
    Model 41, 160
    Model 52, 158
Springfield
    .45, 154
    Loaded Model .45, 92
    LW, 56, 119, 187
    LW Operator, 233
Taurus
    .22, 149
    24/7, 124
    82, 141
    M 44, 132
    Tracker, 138
Tokarev, 54–56
    TT 33, 52
Walther, 190, 200
    P1, 119, 199
    P22, 148, 154
    P38, 49, 53, 152
    Police Pistol, 57
    PPK, 154
Webley .455, 208
Para Ordnance, 191
Parker, Todd, 61
parts, action, 77–80
Patton, Gen. George S., 14, 30
revolver, 73–83, 87
    .22 Magnum, 174, 176
    .357 Magnum, 88, 136, 147, 172,
        174, 177
    .38, 40
    .38 Special, 162, 174, 245
    .38-44, 42
    .44 Magnum, 4, 81, 137, 147, 169–170,
        172–173, 176–177, 241
    .44 Russian, 177
    .44 Special, 42, 173–174, 191
    .44-40-caliber, 11
    .454, 81
    .454 Casull, 173, 176–177

Adams and Deane, 35
Allen and Thurber, 35
Beretta Stampede, 26
cap-and-ball, 23
Charter Arms, 80
  .44 Special, 77
  .44 Special Bulldog, 81
Colt, 21–22, 26, 35, 37, 73, 77, 100
  .22, 42
  .22 Magnum, 22
  .31, 23
  .357 Magnum, 29–30
  .36, 23
  .38, 37, 40
  .38 Special, 22
  .41, 45
  .44, 23
  .44-40, 26
  .44 Magnum, 24
  .44 Special, 28
  .45 ACP, 24
  .45, 24, 26, 28–30, 32, 37, 39, 88–90,
  172, 175, 191, 241–242
  .455, 82
  1892, 101
  Ananconda, 171
  Army Model, 10
  Army Special, 45
  cap-and-ball, 11–12
  Central Fire .45, 14
  Detective Special, 43, 45–46
  Frontier, 100
  Frontier Double Action, 36
  Model 1892, 45
  Navy .36, 30
  New Frontier Single Action .22,
  153–154
  Official Police (COP), 35–36, 38,
  44–46, 155
  Police Positive, 45
  Python, 46, 77
  single-action, 33, 150
  Single Action Army, 13, 15, 41, 175
CZ 52, 137
Dan Wesson, 204
Dixie Gun Works, 232
double-action, 23, 29, 35–46,
  137–138, 203
Enfield, 39
H&R .38, 13
Heckler & Koch .32 Magnum, 74
High Standard Double Nine, 167

Les Baer Monolith, 163
Luger, 41
Magnum, 232
Mauser, 53
  1891, 54
Nagant, 137
Navy Arms 44-40, 22
  Deluxe, 26
  Deluxe SAA, 13
North American Mini Revolver, 136
reloading, 82–83
Ruger, 26, 29, 73, 209–210, 231
  .22, 128
  .357 Magnum, 32
  .41 Magnum, 32
  .44 Magnum, 32
  .480, 74
  Blackhawk, 30–31
  Blackhawk .357 Magnum, 31
  Magnum, 82
  Montado, 30, 33
  Single Six, 137, 153
  single-action, 30–33
  Super Blackhawk, 30, 32, 73
  Super Blackhawk .44 Magnum,
  32, 175
  Vaquero, 33
SIG SAUER, 26
  P220, 87
single-action, 9, 21–34
  operating basics, 99–
Smith & Wesson, 36–37, 40, 73, 77–79,
  94, 100, 105, 195, 212–213, 238
  .32, 36–37
  .357 Magnum, 42–43, 79, 141, 151,
  195
  .38, 12, 36, 39, 100, 209
  .38 Special, 40, 44
  .40, 191
  .44 Magnum, 43, 45–46, 195
  .44 Special, 37
  .45, 39, 173
  .45 Auto Rim, 82
  .455, 82
  .460, 169
  .500 Magnum, 169
  .629 .44 Magnum, 78
  break-top, 25
  center-fire, 138
  Chief's Special, 43–45
  Combat Magnum, 42, 46, 86
  Combat Masterpiece, 41

Hand Ejector, 40, 101
K 22, 167
K 38, 41–42
Magnum, 74, 169
Military and Police (M&P), 40–41,
    44–46, 93
Model 12, 41, 44
Model 25, 169
Model 27, 38, 43, 46
Model 29, 46
Model 442, 80
Model 625, 90
Model 629, 91
Model Ten, 40
N, 172
Perfected Model, 16
Triple Lock, 101
X-frame, 169
Springfield 1911, 163
Sturm Ruger, 27
swing-out cylinder, 137
Taurus, 73, 80
    .357 Magnum, 83
    .44 Magnum, 74–76, 89
    .454 Casull, 74
    double-action, 39
    Judge, 41
    Model 85, 195
    Raging Bull, 81
    Tracker, 83, 138–139, 170, 195, 213
trigger-cocking, 35
Uberti, 14, 26
Ultra Lite, 90–91
United States Firearms (USFA), 26, 28
    .45, 31
    Rodeo, 22, 175, 238
Webley, 17, 37, 39–40, 73, 100, 202
    .455, 39, 82
    Mark VI, 39
Winchester lever-action, 47
.38 Hand Ejector, 31
recoil, 80
rifle
    .44 Magnum, 177
    Sharps, 11
    Taylor and Company 1874 Sharps, 169
Rock River Arms, 160

Ruger, Bill, 31
Ruger, 191
safety
    children around firearms, 120
    gunhandling, 119–120
    handling the pistol, 116–119
    holster, 120–122
selecting a handgun, 190–195
shooting
    combat, 183–188
    competition, 157–
        bull's-eye, 157–160
    fast draw, 167
    in motion, 188–189
    Practical Police (PPC), 167
    presentation, 189
    recreational, 148–155
    silhouette, 165–167
SIG SAUER, 191
Smith & Wesson, 13, 191, 193
    AirLite .44, 91
    Model 66 .357 Magnum, 35
Springfield, 62, 191
stance, 131–132, 181–182
    boxer, 132, 185
    bull's-eye, 185
    dueling, 185
    isosceles, 132, 182
    Weaver, 129–130, 132, 180–182, 187
        modified, 130, 185
Taylor and Company, 11
technique, Applegate, 187
Threepersons, Tom, 231
Thomas, Heck, 14
Travis, Merle, 123
vest
    Classic Old West Styles (COWS), 233
    concealed-carry, 233
Villa, Pancho, 166
W. C. Wolff, 26
Wagoner, Eddie, 92
Wainwright, Gen., 14
Wesson, Dan, 80
Williams, Ralph Hunt, 232
Winchester, 9
Wood, J. B., 201